# Enjoying God's Beauty

# Enjoying God's Beauty

John Navone, S.J.

*A Liturgical Press Book*

**THE LITURGICAL PRESS**
Collegeville, Minnesota

Cover design by Ann Blattner. Illustration: Sano di Pietro's *Madonna of Humility,* reproduced by Chiara Perinetti Casoni and photographed by Bruno Mazza, Rome.

| 2 | 3 | 4 | 5 | 6 | 7 | 8 | 9 |
| --- | --- | --- | --- | --- | --- | --- | --- |

**Library of Congress Cataloging-in-Publication Data**

Navone, John J.
    Enjoying God's beauty / John Navone.
       p.   cm.
    "A Liturgical Press book."
    Includes bibliographical references.
    ISBN 0-8146-2486-3 (alk. paper)
    1. God—Beauty.  I. Title.
BT153.B4N39   1999
231'.4—dc21
                                                    98-35029
                                                       CIP

# Contents

# Introduction

## I

This book is about the joy of seeing the beauty of God in our lives. Both Christian faith and contemplation entail the joy of seeing God's beauty in our lives.

The threefold approach of this book to the joy and beauty of God in Christian life begins with an overview of the Christian experience of beauty. Some basic assumptions for this overview follow.

Wherever there is Christian life, there is Christian vision and action. Christian action is always an expression, however implicit, of Christian vision. The pouring of God's love into our hearts through the gift of his Holy Spirit (Rom 5:5) transforms the cognitive-affective consciousness that constitutes our vision. The Spirit of Christ's love transforms our vision and action into loving Christian vision and action, enabling us to share the "look of love" with which the Father beholds his Beloved Son (Mark 1:11; 9:7). Christ's giving sight to the blind is a metaphor for his enabling our true vision of the beauty of that love which is the joy of our salvation. Both the "eye of love" that is Christian faith (according to Lonergan)[1] and the "look of love" that is Christian contemplation represent the way Christ has given sight to the blind.

The Church's Scriptures offer a second approach to our enjoying the beauty of God in our lives. They serve as a matrix for learning both to recognize and to enjoy the goodness of God in all

[1] Bernard Lonergan, *Method in Theology* (New York: Herder and Herder, 1970) 117.

things. The Church employs its Scriptures for helping us to become the friends of God and of one another under the sovereignty of his love. The Bible serves the Christian community not so much as a book to be read, but as scriptural iconography for contemplating its Lord with both "the eye" and "the look" of love.

The Church invites us to contemplate in its scriptural iconography true images of God, ourselves, and the world. Vision, including all the images associated with it, is integral to our motivation and action; it shapes our lives. Truly good lives imply true vision. Through its scriptural iconography, the Church calls us to contemplate the beauty of God's true goodness in Jesus Christ, God's perfect image, that we might become living icons of the same beauty for others.

The very language of the New Testament is alive with the concreteness, imagery, and joy of a people who experience something of the compelling beauty of the risen and glorified Christ. It is the language of life, love, light, truth, joy, glory, praise, hope, faith, and thanksgiving. It is the language of people who have seen (and continue to see) the glory of God, and who experience the joy of life in God's presence.

Our experience of life in the Church offers a third approach to our enjoying the beauty of God. Both Thomas Aquinas and Jonathan Edwards have worked out theologies of beauty based on their experience of that beauty within the community of Christian faith. The worship/liturgy of the Church also bears witness to our communal experience of God's beauty. Finally, the healing and integrating Spirit of God's radiant love within the Church and the world invites reflection on the universal scope of Beauty Itself (God).

## II

> . . . prayer, the "love of beauty" *(philokalia),* is caught up in the glory of the living and true God.
>
> *Catechism of the Catholic Church* § 2727

Catholic theology, philosophy, and spirituality have long taught that the joy of Christian contemplation is to delight in the splendor of the divine love for us in all things.

True beauty, like true friendship, is always a joy for others. Christians who are a true joy for others are, inevitably, experiencing the beauty of God's true goodness and are communicating it as God's radiant icons. There is no discussion of the mediating function of human persons in the communication of God's joy and love. We can love only because we have been loved and enjoyed: this is a psychological as well as theological truth. We are not only called to love Christ in others but to be also the media through which Christ himself loves them. One may wonder how much the success of Paul's or John's preaching was due to the attractiveness of their personalities.

A renewed stress on the mediation of God's joy to the heart through the beauty of his love would dethrone the role of conceptual teaching from its claim to be the sole medium by which the Christian message is proclaimed and regain for us a greater appreciation of the role of parents, friends and significant others in our learning to become the friends of God.

If contemplation is not to be considered a superior calling of some Christians but as the call proper to all, then it follows that neglect of the beautiful will lead to inauthenticity both on the human and the religious levels. One will never convince anyone of the truth of the gospel if one relies upon conceptual clarity alone.

Aquinas affirmed that the delightful beauty and true lovableness of the Son of God draws us to the Father (*In Ioann.* 6, *lect.* 5). For Aquinas, Christ himself is the love of truth and the truth of goodness, so that it is in the beautiful that one comes nearest to grasping what is proper to the Son (*ST* Ia, q. 39, a. 8c; IIa–IIae, q. 145, a. 2c et ad 1m.). It is surely, for Aquinas, our openness to the beautiful which is that interior instinct whereby God touches our hearts and draws us to Godself (*In Gal.* c. 1, *lect.* 4).

The transcendentals of the true, in the form of orthodoxy, and the good, in the form of moralizing, meet with a resistance that does not hold for the beautiful. If rationalist Christians are reductionist in assuming that reason alone suffices for the communication of the gospel message, moralizing Christians are reductionist in assuming that ethics alone suffices. It is rather the beauty of truly believing, loving, and joyful Christians that captivates, motivates, and transforms others. It is the radiant beauty of what is true and good in the gospel message that disarms and charms and transforms us. We cannot know Jesus Christ in the biblical sense without enjoying the beauty of his true goodness. To enjoy him is to know him as the beauty of the Father's way and truth and life for us.

Jesus' giving sight to the blind is a metaphor for his giving us the Holy Spirit of his love which enables our enjoyment of God's beauty with the "eye of love" which is Christian faith and the gaze of love beholding the beloved which is contemplation. The crucified and risen Christ gives us the Holy Spirit of his life, love, joy, truth, and peace in the triune communion-community-communications that beautify all creation as the origin-ground-perfection of its beauty. Through the gift of the Holy Spirit's new creation, we enjoy the beauty of God in all creation.

The reason for joy, although it may be encountered in a myriad of concrete forms, is always the same: possessing or receiving what one loves, whether actually in the present, hoped for in the future, or remembered in the past. One who loves nobody or nothing cannot possibly rejoice, no matter how much one craves joy; for joy is always the response of a lover welcoming what is beloved. The Spirit of God's love poured into our hearts (Rom 5:5) enables the joy of Christian faith and contemplation. Our happiness is only as great as our capacity for contemplation: our loving awareness of the divine ground and goodness of the universe. There is no festivity or having a truly "good time" without an element of contemplation. In the present life, for Aquinas (*Summa contra Gentes* 3.37), the utmost happiness takes the form of contemplation: the loving gaze that beholds the Beloved in all things. Creation is willed by God, which means that it was created in love and is, therefore, by its mere existence good and worthy of contemplation. The Holy Spirit enables us to share the joy of God in contemplating the beauty of God's goodness in all creation.

The loving gaze that beholds the beloved, contemplation, is concerned about what we enjoy. Augustine distinguished between the things that we employ and other things that we enjoy yet cannot and must not employ/use. To enjoy a thing means to accept it for itself and to find joy in it. To use a thing means to make it a means to obtain what we enjoy. True friends find joy in one another.

Their joyful regard for one another expresses the way that they behold one another. The joy of true friends entails their experience of beauty in its original meaning as the glow of the true and the good irradiating from every ordered state of being (and not in the patent significance of immediate sensual appeal).

The joy of contemplation is the joy of divine and human love in friendship. There is no contemplation without love. Friendship, for Aquinas, is the aim and fulfillment of all human and divine law: "[T]he purpose of the great commandment is charity; since every law aims at establishing friendship, either among human persons, or between them and God, therefore the whole Law is comprised in this one commandment, 'Thou shalt love thy neighbor as thyself,' as expressing the purpose of all commandments" (*ST* I–II, q. 99, a. 1, ad. 2); "[T]he primary aim of human law is to create friendship among human persons" (*ST* I–II, q. 99, a. 2); "Charity is friendship . . . since there is a communication between ourselves and God, inasmuch as He communicates his happiness to us, some kind of friendship must needs be based on this same communication, of which it is written (1 Cor 1:9): 'God is faithful, by Whom you are called unto friendship of his Son.' The love which is based on this communication is charity: therefore it is clear that charity is friendship of ourselves for God" (*ST* I–II, q. 23, a. 1); "Charity is a certain friendship of ourselves for God through which we love God and God loves us; and thus there is effected a certain association of ourselves with God" (III *Sent.* d. 27, q. 2, a.l.; cf. *ST* I–II, q. 28, a. 1); "[F]riendship consists in communication" (*In Eth.* 1658); "[M]utual love is prescribed to us by divine law" (III *Contra Gentiles* c. 117); "[I]t is impossible to have charity without faith and hope. Charity signifies not only the love of God, but also a certain friendship with Him; which implies, besides love, a certain mutual return of love, together with mutual communion, as stated in *Ethics* viii. This is clear in 1 John 4:16: 'He who abides in charity abides in God, and God in him' and from 1 Cor 1:9 (above). Now this friendship of ourselves with God, which consists in a certain familiar colloquy with Him, is begun here, in this life, by grace, but will be perfect in the future life by glory; and both these things we hold by faith and hope. Therefore just as friendship with a person would be impossible, if

one disbelieved in, or despaired of the possibility of their fellowship or familiar colloquy; so too, friendship with God, which is
charity, is impossible without faith, so as to believe in this fellowship and colloquy with God, and to hope to attain this fellowship. Therefore, charity is quite impossible without faith and
hope."

Aquinas affirms that the possibility of Christian contemplation
is destroyed by a lack of love (III *Contra Gent.* c. 117):

> Again. In order to apply ourselves to divine things, we need calm
> and peace. Now mutual love, more than anything else, removes
> the obstacles to peace. Seeing then that the divine law directs us
> to apply ourselves to divine things, we must conclude that this
> same law leads us to love one another.

The true contemplation of God finds its matrix in the true peace
of human friendship. The divine and human communion, community, and communications in friendship is the dynamic of peace or
*shalom* that makes possible the joy of contemplation. The gospel
message tells us that our friendships are not mere incidents or
side issues to the main problems of human existence; rather, we
live our lives for our friendships; they are the goals, not the means
for the joy of that contemplation which culminates in the "seeing
that confers happiness" forever. True friendship is the foretaste
and beginning of that perfect joy; for, even now, the sight of
someone we love makes us happy.

The way we envision God is always determined from the start
by the way we love and treasure the *things* around us. It is, as Karl
Rahner has affirmed,[2] not as if we first of all knew God in a *neutral* fashion, subsequently considering whether to adopt a loving
or hating attitude toward God. Such neutral knowledge of vision,
such "objectivity," is a philosophical abstraction. It is impossible
to be neutral in the face of God and God's creation; for human
experience is always both cognitive and affective. Our concrete
knowledge or vision of God is born of the love or lack of love
with which we relate to the persons and things presented to us
within the context of our life's story.

[2] *Hearers of the Word* (London: Sheed & Ward, 1969) 106.

In Plato's *Symposium* Diotima expresses the traditional wisdom that identifies human happiness with the contemplation of divine beauty: "This is that life above all others which man should live, in the contemplation of divine beauty; this makes man immortal" (*Symposium* 212a. Jowett's translation, modified). Whenever we succeed in bringing before the mind's eye the hidden goodness of everything that is, we succeed in having a "good time." Festivity is always a union of peace, intensity of life, and contemplation: the enjoyment of what is meaningful in itself. Chrysostom grasped the meaning of festivity: "Where love rejoices, there is festivity."[3] Our lives of Christian faith and contemplation are festive. In the midst of our daily cares we gaze into the loving face turned towards us, and in the splendor of that face we see everything which is, is good, worthy of love, and loved by God.

Just as there is no joy without love, there is no contemplation without beauty; for, to paraphrase Stanislaus Fumet in *Procès de l'Art,* beauty is goodness making a spectacle of itself so that it may be loved. The power of beauty moves us to that look of love beholding the beloved which is contemplation.

\*   \*   \*

. . . Beauty, for the scholastics, was a transcendental: it was, that is to say, something which pertained to each and every existent in so far as it existed at all. It might be more or less deficient of beauty, as of goodness and unity and truth: but in so far as it existed at all it must share in some measure in all these. Without them it would not exist at all. The beauty of a thing is a mark of its reality; to be struck, caught by the beauty of a body, or a building or a picture is to be transfixed by its reality, to be attracted to it, captivated. Beauty, for the scholastics, was encompassed by two sets of concepts: on the one hand those related to the words *formosa, speciosa,* concerned precisely with form, with the order and proportion, the rightness of a body, a work of art, a scene; and on the other those related to the word *splendor,* the beauty that shines forth from the object of beauty, and which transfixes and

[3] Cited in Louis de Thomassin, *Traité des festes de l'Eglise* (Paris, 1683) 2:21.

transforms those who behold and *see* it. It is the form, the *Gestalt,* which gives expression to the artist's vision; and yet the splendour of that vision, the glory which shines forth, is nowhere present except in the form. That is to say, the beauty of a picture is neither a particular aspect of it, nor something over and above the work of art itself, to which the work merely points; the beauty is in the work itself in the manner in which the individual passages of the picture are "formed" together by the artist's vision; in the rightness of the artist's choice of color, composition, texture, and the like. The work itself is a wonder, not something we can fully explain, but which we can only contemplate, admire, be captivated by.[4]

[4] John Riches, "Von Balthasar as Biblical Theologian and Exegete," *New Blackfriars* 79 (293) (January 1998) 40.

# Part I

CHRISTIAN EXPERIENCE OF BEAUTY

# 1

# Windows on Beauty

## Theological Presuppositions for *Enjoying God's Beauty*

There are presuppositions that underlie every theology and spirituality. Although not exhaustive, the following survey of presuppositions for *Enjoying God's Beauty* is useful.

1. God is Happiness Itself (Aquinas, *Summa Theologiae,* I–II, q. 3, a. 2). "Perfect happiness belongs by nature to God alone, as in him being and happiness are identical. For the creature, however, perfect happiness is not a natural possession but its last end" (*ST* I, q. 62, a. 4). God's very being is God's being happy. Whatever God is, is God's happiness; this is not something extrinsic to God, but the very life or eternal activity of God.

2. Communion, community, and communication with God is communion, community, and communication with Happiness Itself. The friends of God know, even now but not fully, the happiness that is God. Their faith and hope and love are, even now, an experience of Happiness Itself.

3. Happiness Itself is the interpersonal unity of communion, community, and communications of the triune God's knowing its truth, loving its goodness, and enjoying/delighting in the beauty of its true goodness. The friends of God, therefore, participate even now in the happiness that is God's knowing and loving and enjoying.

3

4. Jesus Christ's affirmation that he is "the way and the truth and the life" (John 14:6) implies that all who welcome the gift of his Holy Spirit are on the way to the life of what is truly Happiness Itself. Eternal life, eternal love, eternal truth and eternal happiness express the universal grace and call of Jesus Christ to enjoy forever Happiness Itself.

5. Knowing God, in the biblical sense, entails our being able to "see" and to "love" and to "enjoy" and to "obey" God within the historical particularities of our daily lives. The persons who "know" God praise, thank, adore, and petition God. The German phrase *Leben ist Loben* ("To live is to praise") expresses the biblical idea of what it means to be fully alive. Persons incapable of finding anything in their lives for which they can thank and praise God are not fully alive.

6. The dogma of creation, based on the biblical revelation that God is the Creator, the Origin and Ground and Destiny of all creation, is the basis for the Christian contemplation of God in all things. Our belief in creation presupposes the communion of the Creator's mind/heart and the human creature's mind/heart—two knowing and loving subjects—in whatever is real. The "informed" or imitating knowledge of us humans is always a participation in the absolutely creative and inventive knowing of the Creator. All things are thought by their Creator and, therefore, knowable to the human mind. All things are willed/loved by their Creator and, therefore, can be loved by the human heart. All things are enjoyed by their Creator and, therefore, can be enjoyed by knowing and loving human subjects. The revelation that God is the Creator of all things is the basis for our affirming the truth (knowability) and goodness (lovability) and beauty (delightfulness) of all things. Belief in creation presupposes an implicit communion of God and humankind in truly knowing and truly loving and truly enjoying/delighting in whatever is real. That the Creator has first known, loved, and delighted in all things endows all things with communicability as divinely and humanly knowable, lovable, and enjoyable. This is the twofold orientation/relativity of all things as divine gift and call for communion in our

knowing the truth, loving the goodness, and enjoying/delighting in the beauty of all things.

7. God created the universe, as Aquinas affirms (*In Div. Nom.,* c. 4, *lect.* 5, n. 349), to make it beautiful for Godself by reflecting God's own beauty. Out of love for the beauty of God's own true goodness, God gives existence to everything, and moves and conserves everything. Beauty Itself (God) intends everything to become beautiful within the fullness of its own true goodness. Insofar as God as Happiness Itself knows God's truth, loves God's goodness, and delights in/enjoys the beauty of God's true goodness, God's creating the universe to be beautiful means that God has created it to be enjoyable/delightful.

8. God sees what God has made, and it is good because God sees it and sees it as good. God's vision/love/delight is not a response to created truth/goodness/beauty; it is the cause of their truth/goodness/beauty.

9. *Splendor formae,* as an aspect of beauty, can be understood within the context of the biblical revelation. We reflect the beauty of God's true goodness when we *conform* to it. Because God's will for us is always God's love for us, our conformity reflects the beauty of God's love for us. Self-will in opposition to God's will/love for us is a *deformation/deformity* (ugliness) of what had been created as a true image and likeness of God. Jesus Christ saves the world by *transforming* the *deformed,* by *transfiguring* the *disfigured,* through the gift of his Holy Spirit of love. The triune God's self-gift, the Holy Spirit of the Father and of the Son, enables us to reflect the beauty of God's true goodness.

10. Jesus' giving sight to the blind in the gospel narratives is a metaphor for his being the enabler of our true vision. Through the gift of his Spirit, we are empowered with the "eye of love" that is faith to see and to delight in the beauty of God, even now, within the concreteness of our human life story. Jesus' giving sight is, therefore, a liberation from the blindness of that unfaith and unlove that precludes our enjoying God. Jesus' giving sight/faith is always Jesus' giving the joy of Happiness Itself.

11. Contemplation is "the look of love." The Creator contemplates creation with the love that constitutes its goodness. Jesus inaugurates the new creation with the same look of love that constitutes our goodness as the sons and daughters of God, as the children of light. The literary structure of the Synoptic Gospels discloses a recurrent pattern in which Jesus contemplates/views a human situation, says something about it, and transforms it to bring joy and happiness. Jesus' contemplating humankind is always his loving humankind with the transforming power of Happiness Itself. His "look of love"/contemplation enables ours in reciprocity. In his sight, we have sight; in his light, we have light; in his love, we become lovely and loving.

12. Mark's Gospel implies the link between God's look of love and the mission of the Son. Both at Jesus' baptism and transfiguration he is recognized and affirmed as the Beloved Son in whom God delights. His Father's look of love empowers him to inaugurate his mission at his baptism for the transformation/beautification of all humankind into a community of beloved sons and daughters sharing that love. On the Mount of the Transfiguration, Jesus radiates the transforming beauty that he reflects from his Father's look of love. Through the power of his transfigured and transfiguring humanity his disciples rejoice in seeing the glory/beauty/splendor of God. Through and in the Beloved Son we are transfigured/transformed by the Father's love and delight in us. We can now "hear" with the Beloved Son that we, too, are beloved; we can now experience with the Beloved Son the Father's delight/joy in us. We now radiate the beauty of God's love and joy.

13. If the beautiful, as Aquinas asserts, is "that which when seen gives pleasure," the "seeing" and "pleasure" or "delight" of God in God's beauty is not physical; for "God is spirit" (John 4:24). Both the divine and human "seeing" and "pleasure" or "delight" in beauty entail the cognitive and affective consciousness of knowing and loving subjects. The experience of beauty is primordially spiritual. Beauty Itself, the origin and ground and perfection of all created beauty, is Spirit; and the transcendent Spirit of God is equally supreme goodness and truth. Being material/physical is not a *sine qua non* for being good or true or beautiful.

14. Joy always accompanies the experience of beauty. The beautiful is enjoyable or delightful. That joy which the world can neither give nor take away from us, analogously, accompanies our experience of God's beauty. The delight/joy that the Father has in beholding the Beloved Son in Mark's accounts of Jesus' baptism and transfiguration implies that the beauty of the Son transcends merely human beauty. Similarly, the joy that Jesus has in his Father implies his experience of a beauty that transcends time and space. Joy, as a fruit of the Holy Spirit, always evidences the experience of God's beauty: the splendor of God's self-giving love and goodness.

15. The faith whereby we enjoy the beauty of God in our experience of our basic self-others-world-God relationship has a relative as well as an absolute aspect; for it apprehends all things in the light and shadow of that transcendent self-giving Love. In the shadow, for that transcendent Love is supreme and incomparable. In the light, for that transcendent Love transforms, magnifies, and glorifies all things within its all-encompassing goodness. The triune God is not a part of creation; rather, as Truth/Goodness/Beauty Itself, God transforms, magnifies, and glorifies it.

16. Just as there is a distinction between our true good and an apparent good, there is a distinction between true beauty and seductive beauty. True beauty, like our true good, is experienced in whatever attracts us to our true fulfillment and happiness. Seductive beauty entails whatever allures us to our self-destruction (morally or spiritually). The same distinction holds between the prudent and the clever person. Although both have a talent for knowing the means for achieving their ends, the former is moral (virtuous) and the latter is immoral. Similarly, there are true solutions and pseudo-solutions to problems; there are true and apparent friends.

17. The New Testament conversion concepts of *metanoia* (personal transformation), *kenosis* (generosity), *diakonia* (service), and *koinonia* (fellowship) are all related to the joy of experiencing God's beauty in Christ's self-giving love which transforms our hearts and minds, inspiring us to become self-giving persons

who serve others in the commitment of that love which reveals that we are truly Christ's disciples (John 13:35). The beauty of our love reveals the beauty of Christ's and the Father's Holy Spirit of love that unites us in communion, community, and communications (*shalom*/peace/friendship). Conversion as both event and lifelong process manifests the beauty of God's true goodness in making the world beautiful.

18. The Good Shepherd metaphor in John's Gospel contributes to our understanding the transforming impact of God's beauty in human life. *Kalos* is both the word for "beautiful" and "good" in describing the beauty of Jesus' laying down his life for his sheep and the goodness of that life for them (10:11). The beauty of the Shepherd's self-giving love explains how Jesus, like God, the Shepherd of Israel, leads, draws, attracts, unites, and sustains his sheep. The splendor of the Beautiful/Good Shepherd on the cross will draw all persons to himself (12:32). The beauty of God's self-giving love in the crucified and risen Christ saves us by drawing us to itself. This is the implicit truth of Dostoyevsky's affirmation that "Beauty saves the world." Drawn by the transforming beauty of the Shepherd, we leave our ugliness behind. The Beautiful/Good Shepherd fulfills the expectations of Israel (Ps 15:11):

> You will show me the path of life,
> the fullness of joy in your presence,
> at your right hand happiness forever.

19. In the Fourth Gospel, Jesus is above all the revealer of God (1:18), and reveals God by manifesting in creation and in human history the "glory" of God so fully and completely that in Jesus "the Word became flesh and dwelt among us" (1:14). The "glory" of God in this gospel is a matrix for understanding the beauty of God in Christian life. The "glory" that inspires Jesus' life and mission is that of his Father (7:18; 8:50, 54; 9:24; 11:4, 40; 12:28, 43; 13:31). Jesus is the obedient Son of the Father who sent him; he works as he sees the Father working (5:19) and speaks what his Father tells him (8:26-28). The supreme "work of God" that Jesus accomplishes is his passion and death. John identifies

Jesus' passage back to God through his death and resurrection as his "glorification" and as the supreme revelation of God's "glory," that is, the effective presence of God's self-giving love in the world (7:39; 12:16, 23, 28; 13:31; 17:5). The notion of "glory" in the Fourth Gospel is in the nature of a synthesis of all the Johannine expressions for the revelation and communication of God's love.

20. A Catholic understanding of joy in God's beauty is grounded in basic Catholic doctrines concerning creation, providence, eschatology, revelation, christology, soteriology, pneumatology, the Trinity, and incarnation.

21. Beauty is at the heart of all human motivation. True beauty as the attractiveness of the truly good motivates human life and development in that intellectual, moral, and religious self-transcendence that constitutes human authenticity or excellence. Without our experiencing the attractiveness or beauty of intellectual, moral, and religious goods, such goods are bereft of their power to transform our lives. Beauty is the enabling power of the truly good to draw us out of ourselves for the achievement of excellence. The bias which regards beauty as ornamental, cosmetic, and useless overlooks the indispensable motivational power of beauty for the attainment of human excellence and happiness. Always treasure whatever moves/inspires you, because you will never accomplish anything in life with what does not. Ultimate Reality (God) calls or beckons us in what we find most beautiful. Our personal vocation is rooted in our experience of beauty. Significantly, the Greek word for beauty *(ton kalon)* comes from the Greek verb *kaleo,* which means to call or beckon. True beauty is the attractiveness of whatever is truly good for us.

22. There is no truly human life without beauty. If beauty is at the heart of human decision and action, a life without it would be unmotivated, mere drift, and less than human. There is no human adherence, commitment, or genuine achievement apart from the sustained experience of beauty. Our need for beauty is felt in the most basic demands of the human mind and heart. Beauty is the power of the good to command, focus, and sustain the attention

necessary for our becoming intelligent, reasonable, responsible, and loving. It is the power to motivate and to sustain inquiry and understanding, reflection and judgment, deliberation, evaluation, decision, and action.

23. The creative power of Beauty Itself (God) is reflected in the procreative power of human beauty in sexual attraction. The reciprocal attractiveness or beauty of male and female is the starting point for most human life stories. Human existence itself evidences the life-giving power of divine and human beauty. To be or not to be is a question of beauty and its motivating power.

# 2

# In a Glass Darkly

There are diverse and apparently paradoxical ways in which we may be, at least implicitly, aware of the presence of God.

Our experience of time in *prayer* is one way of enjoying God's time and of transcending our own. Prayer is a way of learning to live in God's time. God has time for everyone. The call to "pray always" is a call to live in God's time for everyone with the grateful realization that God's time is God's self-gift for everyone. Prayerfully living in *God's* time, we do not reward others—divine or human—as taking or consuming *our* time. We are free from the illusion that the only time that we have is our own. Some seldom find time to pray because they are living in their own time and do not want to lose it for God or for others. Ironically, they know that their time is limited or running out. Prayer is a form of life in God's time and love for everyone. Prayer expresses the gift of that time and love which endure forever.

Prayer, in terms of the Greek distinction between *chronos* (time as perpetual slavery to the circle of routine and repetition) and *kairos* (time as the saving intervention or visitation of God), is a liberating participation or communion in the freedom of God's eternal life and love. *Kairos,* the time of salvation, is always the realm of God's eternal life and love; it is always God's gracious self-communication. The coming of Jesus is the great *kairos,* the reign of eternal life and love in humankind. It is the *kairos* of God's self-revelation and triumph over the circular futility of *chronos.* The self-giving of the Father in sending the Son and

11

Spirit is a call to enter into the *kairos* of the triune communion of eternal life and love. The crucified and risen Christ conquers *chronos* to communicate the triune *kairos* to all humankind. Our prayer to the Father in the Spirit of the Son is even now our experience of divine time or divine life and love.

We may be also sharply aware of the implicit presence of God, who alone is good (Mark 10:18), in our experience of *disappointment* with ourselves and others. Our implicit awareness of the Supreme Good and measure of all goodness (God) would seem to be a presupposition for our ability to experience profound disappointment in the way we fall so short of that goodness. The gap between what we are and what we are called to be intimates our dim awareness of the Supreme Good within the light of whose presence we can recognize the gap and experience the pain of disappointment. We are called to the joy of true love or loving others as they truly are: God above all and others as ourselves. We frustrate and disappoint ourselves in loving God for less than what God is, the Supreme and Absolute Good who alone can satisfy the human heart. Our attempts to love others or ourselves above all frustrate us, for we are not absolutely lovable. Self-idolatry precludes the joy of loving the limited, finite, relational persons that we are. The human ego is not the Supreme Good or ultimate context of all human life, despite our futile attempts to act as though it were. The disappointment that results from our failure to love truly bespeaks the abiding presence of the Supreme Good with which we are in conflict.

We experience the presence of God in the *question-raising Mystery* (God) at the heart of all human life. Questions that arise about our origin and ground and destiny are all implicitly about God. We are not self-explanatory; our meaning and purpose are in some way beyond us. We live in the daily question-raising tension of discovering what God's will is for us. We experience God's presence in our wondering what God wants of us. If our lives are the manifestation of God's grace, they are also measured by the demands of God's intention. Aware of our endless capacity for self-deception, we cannot assume, self-righteously, that we are doing God's will. God alone is unquestionably good. If our desire for God is at the root of our desire for truth, then this desire will not be able to take refuge in illusions. God is the ultimate horizon of truth that continually activates our desire to ask questions and allows us no peace until we have surrendered to it. God is the ultimate objective of all our questioning. We experience this presence in our God-given desire for the truth. The dynamic of the question-raising Mystery (God) underlies all human growth and development. In our questions we experience something of the promise of God; in the answers we experience something of the fulfillment that God alone can give.

Experiencing God as our Supreme Good is a source of *joy;* for joy is always associated with the experience of what is truly good for us. True love brings joy. Paul lists joy among the fruits of the Spirit (Gal 5:22), right after love. As in the case of the Beatitudes, joy always has an affinity with our active commitment to values.

As the Origin and Sustainer and Fulfillment of all human life, God is the joy of all who truly love human life and goodness. The supreme goodness of God is the ultimate possibility of joy available to the human heart. God's joy in loving us grounds our joy in loving God. Jesus invites all to love as he loved in order to share his joy (John 6:10-12).

Everyone seeks joy. The question is, where do you find it? One false assumption is that pleasure is the only way to joy; however, joy and pleasure are not the same. In fact, there is often a tension between them. We never tire of joy, but we easily tire of pleasure. Joy can substitute for pleasure, making us independent of the need for pleasure. Pleasure cannot substitute for joy, nor can it create joy where joy does not already exist. Joy, like all goodness, is outgoing so it is good to be with joyful persons. Someone bent on pleasure is different. The search for pleasure tends to isolate us. The pleasure of the senses cannot substitute for the joy of the spirit; rather, it seems to lead to deeper sadness. Pleasure and joy can coexist and reinforce each other, providing that joy is there already and in a sense prevails. To resolve a moral conflict in favor of pleasure is not necessarily to resolve it in favor of joy. Everyone must find a meaning in life that brings with it, as a side effect, joy. Such joy can exist in the midst of difficulties and privations. On the other hand, misery loves company, so misery can be the root of a desperate search for pleasure.

We are inevitably possessed by God's joy, insofar as we allow this love to take possession of our hearts. The selfishness which limits our capacity for welcoming God's loving goodness into our lives limits also our capacity for true joy. Joy is as much a distinctive mark of the friends of God as peace and love. Such joy does not depend upon a passing success, a moment of triumph; it is, rather, rooted in the joy of God, God's delight in all the human lives that God originates, sustains, and predestines for eternal joy in the Spirit of the mutual, loving recognition and communion of the Father and the Son. The joy God communicates enables us to rejoice in calling God "Abba." We know that the Lord into whose joy we are to enter is here and now our joyful companion. The transformation worked in us by the glory of God, making us capable of recognizing face-to-face the one whom we discern now dimly as in a glass darkly! We are even now gladdened by the thought of what awaits us. The Lord's radiantly joyful recognition of us, "Come, blessed of my Father," will enable us to recognize God with the same joy. In the meantime we are moving towards that fulfillment when we rejoice over everything in the joy of the triune God. We are even now responding to the divine call to enter into the joy of God (Matt 25:21, 23). We are even now finding in God's world traces of the creative joy which brought it into being. We are gladdened by beauty. We know the joy of love and friendship. We rejoice over work well done, over the good fortune of others. Such rejoicing leads us to rejoice in the Source and Sustainer and Fulfillment of joy as a constant in our lives. Because the world does not give this joy, it cannot deprive us of it. Not even death, we believe, can quench the invincible joy of the living God within the hearts of those who love God. Rather, through death we enter into the joy of the Lord.

We are especially aware of the presence of God in those *living icons* whose qualities of mind and heart and action illuminate and inspire us. Their "love, joy, peace, patience, kindness, goodness, trustfulness, gentleness, and self-control" (Gal 5:22-23) communicate what the Spirit of God instills in the lives of God's holy ones. Their love, together with the service which flows from love, is the deepest expression of God's presence within these living icons. Their lives confirm our belief that the Father dwells in the

Son and the Son in the Father, and together with their Spirit, even now, they have come to set up their home in the hearts of all those who believe and accept the word of God (John 14:23). God's indwelling in living icons is a mystery beyond all comprehension. Yet we speak about it, since God has first spoken to us about it. Throughout the ages, the great writers and poets of the Church have constantly attempted to utter the unutterable, employing many metaphors to describe the dynamic intimate presence of the divine three to one another and to the hearts of the righteous.

God's living icons are a beneficent and beneficial presence through whom we experience both the excellence and fulfillment of being loving. Translucent mediators of the God who is Love itself, the light of love shines in the faces of all who encounter them. Their beneficial presence takes the form of ministering to the needs of others just as Christ mediated the love of the Father to all by being present as one who serves (Luke 22:27). Their selfless love and service on behalf of others grounds our conviction that "God is love and anyone who lives in love lives in God, and God lives in him" (1 John 4:16). God's living and loving icons are delightful. Love delights in the presence of the beloved. We know something of God's delight in these loving icons through and in the delight that they take in us. We know the warmth of God's love through our experience of the warmth of their love.

God speaks to us in *whatever deeply moves, motivates, and inspires* us. Our aspirations, hopes, and dreams are the pull of the future in which we experience even now, in a glass darkly, the power of our Origin and Sustainer and Destiny, drawing us to a perfection not yet achieved. We learn to treasure whatever inspires us because we know that we shall never achieve anything in life with what does not, at least in some way, motivate us. Our interests, concerns, and commitments enable us to experience even now something of the God who is guiding us to God's gift of the future. We experience something of God in our desire for human excellence. We know by faith that God wills the excellence of all human persons, and that God inspires the desire for it. We have communion with God, willing what God wills, when we desire human excellence in ourselves and in all others; for our divine Destiny is our divine fulfillment and perfection. God's will for us is always God's love for us and for our excellence. We experience God, the Supreme Good of all humankind, in our desire for what is supremely good for us because God predestines all humankind to communion in the supreme goodness of God's own life. The glory of God is the brotherhood and sisterhood of all human persons in God's Son, Jesus Christ. The Father creates, embraces, and draws all humankind into the splendor of the divine life through the gift of the Son and Spirit in whom we receive our filial and fraternal identity. Ultimately, God inspires and fulfills all human desire. God originates, sustains, and satisfies all human longing. Through faith we experience God as motivating, sustaining, and even now fulfilling our quest for excellence. God is with us from start to finish, from promise to fulfillment. Our existence is always a coexistence with our motivating, sustaining, and fulfilling Origin and Ground and Destiny. Our best efforts are always a collaboration with our self-giving God who provides everything for our ultimate fulfillment.

We experience the difference between our being and our having as our powers are diminished by *aging and dying.* Our powers and possessions gradually slip away, but not our being. We mistakenly tend to identify our being with our having, our significance and self-esteem with our power and possessions. Our tendency to lose ourselves in our power and possessions diminishes our ability to appreciate our being as the gift of our gracious Origin and Sustainer and Destiny. Through the gradual separation of our being from our having, God would save us from losing ourselves (our being) in our distractions (our having). The God who gives all loves and desires all. The God who calls us into being as our Origin and sustains our being as our Sustainer recalls us to Godself as our Destiny. The consolation of aging and dying is that God loves and desires us for Ourselves, for our *being* rather than for our having.

Our dependence on God, our relationship with God, is how we fundamentally are. Our consciousness of this relationship is our sense of God; it may be given, however obscurely, inarticulately, in every sphere of our existence and activity. Our religious tradition is interpretative and transformative of our human experience and knowledge of God. Our encounter with God is not limited to any one particular sphere or level of our experience. God is to be found in all the kinds of things that we do and suffer, achieve, and undergo.

We encounter God in our living and in our dying. The process of dying starts much earlier than the moment of terminal death for our bodily existence which is also constituted by the personal and social relations in which we share. Friends die, relationships wither and, by our failure to communicate and care, our failure to bring each other alive, we contribute to each other's dying. Although our lives seem to terminate with death, there is a sense in which the acceptance of and engagement with mortality is a precondition of coming alive. Unless a grain of wheat. . . . In our relationships with others, with new challenges and situations, we have continuously to be risking the unfamiliar, the disturbing, the unknown. To have life more fully, we must have the courage to risk "dying" throughout our lives. Our maturation and development entail our having the courage to accept the risks involved in accepting our God-given possibilities of coming alive. In the light of the Easter hope, we believe that the human story is ultimately to be told in terms, not of death, but of life, not of absurdity, but of God's invincibly effective love.

God has placed us in the divine presence even before we seek God. Our conscious presence to ourselves is itself the gift of our knowing and loving Origin and Sustainer and Destiny. *Gratitude* for our lives is one form of our response to and communion with our ever-present and sustaining God. The realization that both our being and our having are unmerited gifts inspires a sense of gratitude. Our ability to enjoy anything or anyone is based on our not taking them for granted. Until we realize that they might not be, we cannot fully appreciate them as unmerited gifts. We experience the presence of the Giver in the gifts. Gratitude is our spontaneous response to the Origin and Sustainer and Destiny of our being and having. Our sense that reality is a gift not owed evokes a joyful indebtedness for the gift of ourselves, the world, and others. Joyful appreciation for whatever we are or have reflects our freedom from resentment for not having everything, no less than freedom from indifference. (If human desire can be only partially fulfilled in this life, there always remains a residue of nonfulfillment with the attendant risk of constant resentment; and the surest way to be unhappy is to make our happiness dependent on the fulfillment of impossible conditions.) Gratitude expresses the poverty of spirit of those who welcome God in all God's gifts, recognizing all as gift.

The Christian community, employing its Gospels to awaken us to the presence of God in our lives, proclaims that it has experienced that glorious presence in the suffering servant of God who came to serve rather than to be served. Through the transforming power of the Father's self-giving love in Jesus Christ and the Spirit, the Christian community is the sacred icon or sacrament of the divine community, the glory of the triune God in human history. It expresses both the self-giving and universal call of the triune God to enter into the glory of the divine community, to be as perfect as our heavenly Father is perfect (Matt 5:48), to be as merciful and compassionate towards all as our heavenly Father (Luke 6:36). In words and deeds of compassionate love, the glory of God dispels the darkness from human history. The selfless love of the pure of heart enables them to see and to communicate the glory of God's inspiring, sustaining, and transforming presence. In the light of its crucified and risen Lord and the gift of the Spirit, the Christian community affirms that God is lovingly present and active in every human life story, with an invincible love that evil and death itself cannot quench. In the light of our Easter faith, we see that even now the just are rising through the power of God's transforming love to enter into the fullness of that joy that God has prepared for them. Through the self-giving of the triune God, we even now experience a foretaste of that love that lasts forever.

# 3

# Beauty Begets Beauty

Tuscan landscapes and townscapes are a lesson in beauty. They are lovely because they are loved. Augustine affirmed the link between love and beauty: "Only the beautiful is loved . . . we cannot help loving what is beautiful" (*Confessions* 14.3; *On Music,* 6.13). Siena, in the heart of Tuscany's beautiful landscapes, is famous for its monumental paintings. Interestingly enough, there is a profoundly Christian faith dimension for all this loveliness.

## The Loving Gaze[1]

Environmentalists and Green parties inspire much serious thought about our landscapes. James Howard Kunstler, for example, in *The Geography of Nowhere: The Rise and Decline of America's Man-Made Landscape* deplores the fate of the human habitat in America, which he says has been nearly wrecked by those who occupy it. The destruction of both the natural and the man-made environments will produce "a landscape of scary places, the geography of nowhere, that has simply ceased to be a credible human habitat."

Mr. Kunstler asserts that we are happiest when we inhabit physical surroundings worth caring about, and he says that small-town charm accomplishes this; nothing is more important to the

[1] John Navone, "The Geography of Nowhere Has a Chianti Counterpoint," *International Herald Tribune* (March 8, 1994).

human enterprise than the sense of community that small towns ostensibly encourage.

From atop a tower in a Tuscan village, one sees a landscape that might well realize Mr. Kunstler's ideal. One day, while driving through this magical place, a friend exclaimed to me, "Have you ever seen a landscape that looks so loved, treasured, and cared for?"

Years later, I discovered a basis in history for the well-loved look of Tuscany's Chianti country. The investiture oath of the Chianti League, which was formed at the beginning of the fourteenth century for the administration and defense of the region, begins, "I promise to keep myself close to nature, to give a religious meaning to my life, to look around me with optimism and with love."

Our landscapes and townscapes often reflect inner visions and feelings. The Tuscan landscape, part natural, part husbandry, is lovely because it is loved.

Unfortunately, the devastation of our landscapes and the decay of our townscapes—the ugliness of unloved persons and places and things—often reflect the moral ugliness of our greed, indifference and exploitation. So much of loveliness and beauty is rooted in love itself. Contemplation, the loving gaze that beholds beloved persons, places and things, has much to do with their loveliness. The Creator, according to Genesis, contemplates creation to affirm its goodness; and creation is good because it is affirmed, treasured and cared for.

The possibility of our enjoying anything is based in a kind of humility that takes nothing for granted, recognizing all as a gift. An attitude of entitlement, in contrast, takes things for granted. And when we clamor for more, in continual dissatisfaction, we destroy everything, including happiness.

Our radical acceptance of and gratitude for everything, taking nothing for granted, is part of what the poet Gerard Manley Hopkins called our "inscape," our individually distinctive and fundamental beauty, the precondition for true knowledge and delight. Contemplation is the communion of inscapes.

Tuscan painters, beginning with Ambrogio Lorenzetti in the early fourteenth century, contemplated their landscapes and townscapes. Lorenzetti's frescoes of "Good and Bad Government" in the Siena Town Hall depict the first townscape and landscape in the history of European painting.

Tuscan landscapes seem familiar because they were a favorite background for almost all the Italian painters of the High Renaissance. From Petrarch (1304–74) onward, Tuscan humanists expressed the joy they took in the flora and fauna of the countryside. The pleasure in the countryside expressed in Pius II's "Commentaries" was echoed in his choice of site for his palace at Pienza, with its spectacular view of Monte Amiata. That entire Tuscan towns are as they were four or five centuries ago bespeaks the undying affection of a people for its townscapes.

The Chianti League has given the world some of its most beautiful landscapes and townscapes. With realistic optimism, the Tuscans assume that their ideals can be only partially fulfilled. Rather than focus their attention on the area of nonfulfillment in a state of constant resentment—and the most sure way to be unhappy is to make one's happiness dependent on the fulfillment of impossible conditions—they appreciate their limited Tuscan world, contemplating it with an optimism and love that has led to a strenuous desire to improve it. Their contemplation does not mean passivity. If Tuscany is good, it deserves to be improved. Such basic commitment, like appreciation, takes nothing for granted.

## Siena's Monumental Paintings [2]

The Italian Middle Ages have too often been regarded as simply that—an age "in the middle" between the Roman Empire and

---

[2] My article manuscript, "Siena's Monumental Paintings," was published in two parts with different titles: "Good and bad government" (*The Month,* March 1997) and "The Massa Marittima Maestà" (*The Month,* October 1997). Four chapters of the revised and expanded edition of my book *The Land and the Spirit of Italy: The Texture of Italian Religious Culture* (Brooklyn, N.Y.: Legas, 1998) treat of themes related to the material of this chapter and to Italian iconography in general: Pre-Renaissance Franciscan and Tuscan Humanism (ch. 3); The Transforming Vision of St. Francis (ch. 4); Siena's Icon of the Common Good (ch. 6); Italian Pictorial Art 1300–1600 (ch. 7).

the Renaissance. Such a view not only underrates the vast achievements of these centuries—but makes it very difficult to understand all subsequent Italian history. For Italy as we know it was born in the Middle Ages. The barbarian invasions of the fifth and sixth centuries began a process that turned a unified center of empire into a land of small independent city-states fought over by foreign powers, and so it remained for well over a thousand years. The medieval centuries also saw the growth of a division between the wealthy, politically active north and the poor, politically sub-jugated south. From these political upheavals emerged a charac-teristically Italian localized and urban culture.

By contrast there was one Italian institution that transcended not only regional but even national boundaries—the Catholic Church. The Bishop of Rome was the acknowledged leader of Western Christendom. Theology, when it did not emanate from Italy, was subject to Italian approval. Western monasticism was given its characteristic form by St. Benedict of Norcia and Pope Gregory the Great; and Europe's most influential saint, Francis of Assisi, could have belonged to no other country. Christian iconography and Christian music were also very largely Italian in origin.

## Continuity

The continuing influence of ancient Rome meant that, in a sense, medieval Italy was living on its past. The memory of for-mer greatness never died. In law, in political theory, even in the details of urban living, as much as possible of the classical heri-tage was salvaged and preserved. Even the Church, led by a pope whose title was *Pontifex Maximus,* kept Latin as its language and administered its provinces as a spiritual empire. The influence of the civilizations to the Germanic north and to the Byzantine and Islamic south made Italy the meeting place of ideas, artistic styles, scientific knowledge (as in medicine and physics), and ar-chitectural techniques. What other country could embrace, within one hundred and fifty miles, both St. Mark's in Venice and the Milan Cathedral? A remarkable continuity pervades Italian life and culture. As Virgil could speak to Dante, so Dante can speak to the Italy of today. For here the past never disappears; it merely becomes part of the present.

## Monumental painting

A remarkable development of the Italian Middle Ages was the birth of monumental painting, with Giotto's frescoes at Assisi and the Scrovegni chapel at Padua, Simone Martini's at the Palais des Papes, Avignon, and Ambrogio Lorenzetti's *Allegory of Good and Bad Government* at the Palazzo Pubblico of Siena (1338). Religious painting on wood, influenced by Byzantine and Franciscan spirituality, is represented by Cimabue (1240–1302) in Florence and Duccio di Buoninsegna, who painted the *Maestà* of the Virgin (1311) for the Siena Cathedral.

Sienese art, associated with the names of four great painters and scores of lesser ones, is especially related to the development of monumental painting. A Byzantine streak common to much Italian art runs through Sienese painting. Its telltale signs are rigid attitudes, stiff gestures, elongated and boneless hands, and stylized faces with almond eyes. And although the Byzantine eventually yielded to the Gothic, dominant in Italian fourteenth-century painting, it did not altogether disappear.

Most Sienese painting is religious. But, side by side with piety, there is a showy aspect to Sienese art, favoring elegant clothes, decorative detail, and much gold. Siena's leading painters are Duccio di Buoninsegna (ca. 1255–ca. 1319), Simone Martini (ca. 1283–1344), and the Lorenzetti brothers—Pietro (ca. 1280–ca. 1348) and Ambrogio (ca. 1285–ca. 1348).

Duccio's monumental (13.5 x 7ft.) *Maestà* (Madonna enthroned as Queen of Heaven, surrounded by a court of saints and angels) was finished after thirty-two months of work in 1311, and carried in solemn procession from his studio to the cathedral, whose high altar it decorated for the next 194 years. (It is now in the cathedral museum.) In this grandiose creation, painted on wood, Duccio combines Byzantine rigor with a new, subtle but pronounced humanity and with an elegance of line and strength of color that are his very own. The Virgin is set apart from the packed crowd of grave-faced celestial figures not only by her size but by her soft expression and by the timid tenderness with which she holds the child. Siena had placed herself under the special protection of the Virgin at its victory over the Florentines at Montaperti (1260), and the Madonna was the most painted subject in the embattled city-state.

### "Love justice . . ."

Only four years after the completion of this altarpiece, Simone Martini, his pupil, and his junior by a quarter-of-a-century, painted another *Maestà*—Siena's first major fresco—for the town hall. The spirit of this enchanting work is Gothic. The figures are more lightly posed, more delicately contoured, less powerfully massed, than Duccio's. Grace takes the place of monumentality. The Queen of Heaven seems a queen of Gothic France, listening to the song of troubadours. Two kneeling angels offer her baskets of roses and lilies. The Virgin, as Queen of Siena, sits on her golden Gothic throne and receives the homage of the four kneeling patrons of the city, Saints Ansano, Savino, Crescenzio, and Victor. In the arms of the Virgin the Christ child holds a scroll bearing the words: "Love justice, you who rule the earth."

In a broad band around the picture are metal discs on which appear alternately the arms of the commune (white and black shield) and of the Sienese people (the lion rampant). Below, a verse addresses a moral to the councilors who saw it before them in their deliberations:

> The angelic flowers of roses and lilies with which the heavenly meadow is decked, delight me no more than good counsel. But sometimes I see him who, for his own interest, despises me and deceives my land, and when he speaks it is the worst which is most praised. Let each man watch for him these words condemn.

At the bottom of the picture appears another inscription which the Virgin is supposed to address to the sacred patrons of the city:

> My beloved ones, be assured that I will answer your devout and honest prayers as you would wish, unless the powerful do harm to the weak. Your prayers are not for these, nor for anything which might deceive my land.

With these words the rulers of Siena, "the Nine," had put in the mouth of the Virgin the ideals of their rule: the ideals of polity for the common good over the deceits of private interest.

Siena's Palazzo Pubblico offers a good introduction to the discourse on Italian medieval monumental painting, a pleasing surprise to those arriving from Florence with heads full of Giotto and Fra Angelico. Sienese medieval art speaks to us in ways that Daddis and Gaddis cannot: the narrative romance, the decor, the sinuousness of line, the subtle tricks of color, the affection intrinsic to the manner of masters such as Duccio, Martini, and Ambrogio Lorenzetti.

## Basic Bond of Society

Most famous of all the palace frescoes are those in the Sala della Pace representing the allegorical figures of Good and Bad Government and their respective effects. These were carried out by Ambrogio Lorenzetti between 1337 and 1339 and include some of the most majestic and authoritative concepts of the Italian Middle Ages.

In our modern age of greedy, self-seeking individualism, it is a salutary surprise to find Lorenzetti reflecting St. Thomas Aquinas's philosophy of the common good, the basic bond of society, opposed to ruthlessness, treachery, and discord, ruled by fear, whose descriptive scroll bears the legend:

> Because he looks for his own good in the world, he places justice beneath tyranny. So nobody walks this road without fear: robbery thrives inside and outside the city gates.

In *The Effects of Good Government*, Lorenzetti pioneered the treatment of landscape. In this painting the values of safety, prosperity and unity are embodied by the walled city (clearly identified with Siena itself); they are matched by the peace and order of the neighboring countryside, where peasants till their fields and riders, huntsmen and merchants pass to and fro unmolested. That the Sienese took all this very seriously is proved by, among other things, the sermons San Bernardino preached on the frescoes, giving descriptions which have left us several valuable clues as to interpretation.

Lorenzetti's masterpiece is the most elaborate political allegory which has survived from this century. Stretching over three walls of the *Room of the Nine,* it seeks to give in visual form complete expression to the dominant ideals of the city governors. Lorenzetti's allegory brought together the concepts of the Roman lawyers and the philosophy of such fourteenth-century Thomist-Aristotelians as Giles of Rome, Remigio Girolami, and Ptolemy of Lucca. In its way it is a document of singular importance in tracing the history of the growth of the ideal of the state.

## The Massa Marittima *Maestà*

Bram Kempers (*Painting, Power and Patronage: The Rise of the Professional Artist in Renaissance Italy* [London: Penguin Books, 1994] 146–7) affirms that the *Maestà* was the unique product of circumstances specific to Siena. The special function of the cathedral in civic life was a prime source of innovation. As an altarpiece, Duccio's *Maestà* was unique in that it drew on and integrated different traditions in the visual arts. Duccio's monumental panel, visible to the laity from a great distance, provided a new synthesis of disparate elements whose form and thematic content answered to a particular set of demands. This specificity meant that the *Maestà* was not emulated to any significant extent; still, the number of skills it displayed could be used in any number of contexts. Working on the altarpiece gave Duccio's assistants and pupils the opportunity to master these skills, which expertise they later drew on for smaller commissions executed under the master's supervision and for major orders after Duccio's death in 1318. Their career prospects had been considerably enhanced by their experience in Duccio's workshop.

In the tradition of both Duccio and Simone Martini, Ambrogio Lorenzetti also painted a grandiose and exquisite *Maestà*. His *Madonna and Child enthroned among the Saints* represents Italian iconography at its best. The Palazzo Communale of Massa Marittima is the site of the municipal picture gallery whose chief glory is Lorenzetti's *Maestà,* an opulently conceived triptych,

Ambrogio Lorenzetti's *Maestà* of Massa Marittima (1335), reproduced by
Chiara Perinetti Casoni and photographed by Bruno Mazza, Rome.

painted around 1330. Its presence in Massa Marittima is men-
tioned by both Vasari and Ghiberti.

This Lorenzetti masterpiece is a brilliantly decorative and original interpretation of the theme made famous by Duccio and Simone
Martini. Angels' wings cross to form the back of the Virgin's throne;

the angels uphold the virgin's cushion; on the steps, their colors symbolic, sit personifications of the theological virtues: Faith, Hope, and Charity. There is throughout an emphasis on surface—on the haloes that are like waves of gold, on the bright bands of color that form the steps, on the sparkling dresses of the musician angels.

The *Maestà,* divided into five separate sections, was discovered in 1867 in the monastery of Sant' Agostino in Massa Marittima, stored away in an attic; it was transferred to the Town Hall where it still hangs today. The theological virtues seated at the foot of the throne are reminiscent of the personifications in Lorenzetti's frescoes of Good Government (see *The Month,* March 1997, 107) in the Town Hall of Siena, and may therefore indicate a later date for this painting.

The composition of the *Maestà* is monumental: the Virgin sits on a throne atop three steps, each one painted the same color as the theological virtue seated on it. The name of the virtue is in-scribed on the step: on the lowest one is Faith *(Fides),* dressed in white, looking into a mirror where she contemplates the figures of the Trinity (the dove has almost entirely disappeared); Hope *(Spes),* seated on the second step, painted green, carries a tower; on the third step, red-robed Charity *(Caritas)* bears the flaming heart and bared arrow of love. Six musician angels kneel at the foot of the throne, around which are another four angels, two of whom uphold the Virgin's cushion, and two are casting flowers over the Madonna and child. The rest of the composition is taken up by a throng of patriarchs, prophets, and saints, among whom is St. Cerbone with his geese, the patron saint of Massa Marit-tima. The multitude of haloes is a device taken from the Byzan-tine iconography to indicate a multitude of witnesses.

The flower-throwing angels and the symbolic colors of the steps are reminiscent of Dante's vision of Beatrice, dressed in the three colors of the theological virtues, when she appears to him in Canto XXX of *Purgatory,* "through cloud on cloud of flowers flung from angelic hands and falling down over the cart and all around in showers."

Lorenzetti's striking compositional originality conveys a depth of theological significance. The weighty figure of the Virgin be-comes the apex of a formal pyramid of unprecedented grandeur and solidity. The Virgin embraces her child, bending her face close to his with intense affection, as though she were about to kiss him. The three theological virtues, seated on the massive steps, mark the transition from earth to heaven. Faith lays the foundations of the spiritual edifice; Hope builds on it, and Charity crowns it. A vast body of adoring saints and angels flanks and encloses the Virgin and child—the axis of an imposing compositional triangle. In this pair, thrust cheek to cheek within the protective wings of kneeling angels, Lorenzetti has achieved an almost physical fusion of mother and son that contracts from the multitude of the attending angels who pelt roses and lilies and the unswerving eyes of the ever-watchful crowd. Below the Virgin and Child, on three oval steps, a wraithlike red Charity and her two sister virtues, Faith and Hope, check the observer's access as they form a minor, internal triangle in line with the principle one dominated by the holy couple.

Lorenzetti's subtlety and deliberation in the design of his *Maestà* prefigures similar experiments which later taxed such painters as Masaccio, Leonardo, and Raphael in their handling the depiction of crowds. Lorenzetti's compositional orchestration is so delicate that bank on bank of half-glimpsed heads and haloes seem to bring about the suggestion of infinity, as tiers of heavenly hosts stretch back into the distance. The splendor of tooled gold and the numerous small, broken forms intensify the calm simplicity of the mass, of contour, and of color in the central figure. The color harmony that is based on the steps and theological virtues is as complex and original as the formal structure; both are dominated by the broad, calm areas of the Virgin's dark blue cloak.

Lorenzetti portrays Charity in a diaphanous, close-wrinkled robe of classical style through which the underlying female form is faintly visible. The other two virtues are dressed in medieval costumes. Charity carries an arrow in her hand as well as a heart. Both the classical dress and the arrow are an allusion to Venus, goddess of love. Lorenzetti portrays Charity according to St. Bernard's interpretation: the attribute of the human heart that has been penetrated by the "arrow of divine love." Lorenzetti masterfully seeks to elicit from the viewer of his *Maestà* the gaze of contemplative love and adoration.

The Florentine sculptor Ghiberti (1378–1455) affirmed that Ambrogio Lorenzetti was the greatest painter of Siena and an outstanding designer. Lorenzetti was among the boldest innovators of the experimental generation of artists active in the first half of the *trecento*. He displayed remarkable originality and genius in depicting the relationship between Virgin and Child to which he gave a psychological depth and new naturalistic form impressive both in breadth and form. The serenely maternal manner in which the robust Virgin holds her muscular child reveals Lorenzetti's genius for the subtleties of mother-child interaction never equaled by his contemporaries or followers.

\* \* \*

Contemplation in the classical tradition conveys the notion of looking, gazing, or a way of seeing. The Greek origin of the term is *theorein,* which means to regard or to look at a spectacle or religious event. Some trace the origin of the term back to *theos* (God) while others to *thea* (vision). Both the Greek and the Latin have given rise to common understandings of contemplation as the admiration of beauty, speculative study, or beholding wisdom.

# 4

# Time to Enjoy

What is truth? beauty? friendship? These kinds of questions are conversations about the being of ultimate things. These conversations are leisure: the Aristotelian notion about what you do when you have done everything. Aristotle says that we have to keep alive; we have to eat; we have to have clothes; we have to have shelter; we have to learn to read and to write; we have to control our emotions; we have to become mature adults. But when we have done all that, is there anything left for us to do? What we do is what Aristotle calls leisure. We pursue—in friendship—truth, beauty, love, honor. These things are worthwhile doing. So why should we be bored? We are able to confront ultimate questions and, at the same time, to enjoy the limits and transcendence of leisure.

Reading and conversation are forms of learning and leisure; but they are not the only ways of learning and enjoying leisure. We must test them against other forms, such as films or theater or various forms of art. We ought to pursue or welcome learning and leisure wherever we encounter them.

Not only do we need to read books to learn about ultimate things, we also need to think about these things on our own. We need not merely to know what Aristotle thought about the things, but we need to think through the problem in some organized way, both from our own experience and the experience of the ages. We need to debate these things with our friends. And we can debate them in many ways: in literature, in writing, in speech, in friendship. We can discuss ultimate questions on two levels, intellectually and realistically, in books and in informal conversations.

Leisure is activity that is recreating, humanizing, and divinizing. Leisure leads to wholeness and healing. It is an activity undertaken without calculation of duty or accomplishment: conversation, reading for enjoyment, celebration, prayer, worship, contemplation. Leisure energizes; escapism drains. What is leisure for one person may not be leisure for another. What is leisure one day may not be the next. A worthwhile TV show for one person may be pure escapism for another. A criterion for leisure entails the question: Is this something that I choose to do for its own sake, or is it something to pass the time because I cannot think of anything better to do?

Leisure is not idleness. Leisure and work are complementary. Leisure does not mean an exaggerated focus on self-care that relegates actual work to a distant second place. Leisure's affirmation of all reality includes the affirmation that work gives meaning and dignity to human life. But the affirmation involved in leisure emphasizes as well that work is not all there is to being human, that our humanity is greater than that.

There are forces that work against leisure. Our attitude towards time is one of those. Economists treat time as one more scarce resource to be rationed according to the laws of supply and demand. The economists' approach to time is time as chronological, as measurable, as opposed to "chairotic," as the period during which something important happens. Economists speak of how we "spend" commuting time in order to "buy" living in an area of our choosing. Our ordinary language discloses the influence of the economists' view of time. We spend time, save time, afford time, make time, lose track of time. We talk of time as if it were a valuable possession. *My* time is scarce, *my* time is short, *my* time is money, *my* time is running out. In other words, time has become a commodity, and we are comfortable with the concept of buying and selling time.

Leisure is impossible if I am calculating how much time it will take. Leisure can be described as "spending" time with persons, places, things, and studies that we love. For most people, much of leisure is family time.

If time is a gift, then receiving it freely allows us to give it freely. Leisure can be a way of receiving time gratefully. Joseph Pieper suggests making a "holocaust" of time, returning some of it to God much the way that Deuteronomy 26 mandates the offering of unblemished first fruits of the field and flock, "wasting" it as one does a libation.[1] Finding time for both private and liturgical prayer is a test of our freedom for leisure. If we stop working long enough we may recognize that it is God who holds the universe together and that the universe will continue to work quite well even if we do not.

We have a bias against leisure. We tend to value ourselves in terms of how much work we do and how much money we earn. We live in a culture that values efficiency and productivity above all. Much of our identity and self-worth come from what we do. Our culture values people according to their productivity, which is theoretically reflected in how much money they earn. People who lose their jobs often lose their friends as well. When a job provides identity, what do you talk about with someone who has no job? Our heroes are often tireless workers, activists, and achievers. Leisure is seen as the opposite of work, and work is what human excellence is all about. This way of evaluating ourselves and others permeates our culture. We often pride ourselves on a "realism" that is no different from the high value that our culture puts on productivity and efficiency.

If we come to believe that our work and productivity are the ultimate basis of our value, we shall envision our personal excellence in terms of doing more work and of avoiding anything that appears to be "wasting time." Our actions of caring for people, time spent with friends, and even prayer itself will have no value. The leisure of enjoying God's gifts and of delighting in God's creation become a "waste of time." Our need to be doing and accomplishing can lead to our loss of leisure. The ideal person becomes the one who works constantly, compulsively, and productively. The incapacity for leisure is the incapacity for happiness.

[1] J. Pieper, *What Is a Feast?* (Waterloo, Ontario: North Waterloo Academic Press, 1987) 6.

The Christian tradition sees in leisure the time to build family and societal relationships and an opportunity for communal prayer and worship, for relaxed contemplation and the enjoyment of God's creation, and for the cultivation of the arts which help fill the human longing for wholeness. In the creation narrative God worked six days to create the world and rested on the seventh. That image challenges us to harmonize action and rest, work and leisure, so that both contribute to building up the person as well as the family and community.

Joseph Pieper describes leisure as a mental and spiritual attitude.[2] Compared with the exclusive ideal of work as activity, leisure implies an attitude of non-activity, of inward calm, of silence; it means not being "busy," but letting things happen. Compared with the exclusive ideal of work as toil, Pieper continues, leisure appears in its character as an attitude of contemplative "celebration." Leisure is possible only on the premise that we consent to our own true nature and abide in concord with the meaning of the universe. Leisure stands opposed to the exclusive ideal of work *qua* social function. Leisure does not exist for the sake of work. The point and justification of leisure are not that the functionary should function faultlessly and without a breakdown, but that the functionary should continue to be a human person.

For Pieper, two things are necessary for leisure.[3] It has to be nonuseful, and it must involve some sense of celebration. Leisure is activity that has value in itself, that is not useful for accomplishing some other purpose. Pieper argues against the overestimation of work. He says that we tend to be suspicious of anything that comes without effort: "No pain, no gain." "You have to bear the cross if you want to wear the crown." Pieper sees humans as uncomfortable benefiting from anything they did not earn. As long as they keep working hard, they can try to convince themselves that they have earned what comes their way. Leisure— activity that does not earn anything or involve any calculation of what is coming to whom—breaks out of the work focus and en-

---

[2] *Leisure, the Basis of Culture,* trans. Alexander Dru (Scarborough, Ontario: Mentor, New American Library Mentor-Omega Book, 1963) 40–4.
[3] Ibid., 57.

ables us to recognize that time and all else is gift, not remuneration.

Pieper admits that people cannot be persuaded to engage in something that has no use: "You cannot convert people to leisure by telling them how wholesome and beneficial it is."[4] The heart of leisure is celebration; and we celebrate, not because celebrating is good for us (even though it is), but because life is good. If our conviction is that the world is at root evil, or even neutral, then there is nothing to celebrate. We cannot celebrate without affirming the goodness of the world and assenting to our oneness with the world. In the end, leisure leads to worship. Since leisure presumes celebration of God's presence in all of reality, there is such a close connection between prayer and leisure that encouraging leisure can sound like encouraging prayer.

Many leisure activities, especially those connected with the arts, with nature, and with other people, provide us with experiences of beauty which easily draw us to God; nevertheless, leisure activities by definition have no end outside themselves. We do not pause to enjoy the beauty of art or nature because it will help our prayer later, but because it is beautiful. That such beauty draws us to God is welcome. Our appreciation of the creature implies our appreciation of the Creator. Leisure implicity celebrates the Giver in the gifts of creation. Our capacity for leisure is our capacity for happiness. Leisure is freedom *from* boredom, apathy, and depression; it is freedom *for* joy and celebration.

The call to love God above all and all others as ourselves (Mark 12:28-34 = Matt 22:34-40 = Luke 10:25-28) is a call to divine and human friendship that implies our need for leisure; for the relationship of friendship and its growth require leisure time spent together. Ultimately, we live our lives for our friendships. They are the goals, not the means. Our unwillingness to make or find time for God and others is a self-destructive rejection of our ultimate fulfillment and happiness in divine and human friendship. The generous self-giving and joy of divine and human friendship presuppose our freedom and desire for leisure time together. The leisure for such friendship is a liberation *from* our pathological

---

[4] Ibid., 64.

tendencies to self-absorption, self-pity, and other forms of self-idolatry. It is a liberation *for* enjoying and loving ourselves and others as God does: as we truly are *together with all others* in the triune God. We are together-with-all-others because that is the way the triune God knows/wills/loves us. The graced leisure of divine and human communion-community-communication enables us to know and love and enjoy our true goodness and oneness with all creation and its Creator.

\*   \*   \*

Thornton Wilder's play *Our Town* has for its theme that we never fully appreciate the precious gift of life. *Our Town* implicitly makes a powerful case for the meaning and value of leisure. Emily Webb, after dying in childbirth of her second child, asks if she can relive the happiest day of her life, her twelfth birthday. As her mother is busily preparing for the birthday party, Emily speaks "Oh, Mama, just look at me one minute as though you really saw me. . . . Let's look at one another." And a moment later, she exclaims "it goes so fast. We don't have time to look at one another . . . I didn't realize. So all that was going on and we never noticed." Heartbroken, she realizes that people do not appreciate how beautiful life is. She learns that only the poets and saints appreciate how wonderful life is. Everyone else is too busy.

# 5

# To Enjoy Is to Glorify

The catechism taught that our chief end was to glorify God in this life in order to enjoy God forever. For C. S. Lewis these are the same thing.[1] Fully to enjoy is to glorify. In commanding us to glorify God, God is inviting us to enjoy God. The Great Commandment, in this context, expresses God's invitation to enjoy God with all our being and our neighbor as ourselves.

If the joys of heaven are for most of us in our present condition an acquired taste, then there are certain ways of life that may render the taste impossible of acquisition.

Heaven offers nothing that the mercenary soul can desire. It is safe to tell the pure of heart that they shall see God, for only the pure of heart want to. If we find in ourselves a desire which no experience in this world can satisfy, the most probable explanation is that we were made for another world.

If we let God have God's good way, to utter satisfaction, our place in heaven will seem to be made for us and for us alone, because we were made for it. Jesus affirms that in his Father's house there are many mansions where he is going to prepare a place for us.

Heaven enters wherever Christ enters, even in this life. Christ assures the Good Thief that he shall be with him in paradise: communion, community, and conversation with Christ. The other

[1] *Reflections on the Psalms,* ch. 9, par. 6 (New York: Harcourt, Brace, 1958).

thief in Luke's story of the passion reminds us that if we keep insisting on keeping hell, we cannot enjoy heaven. If we welcome the Spirit of Christ into our hearts, we cannot retain even the smallest and most intimate souvenirs of hell.

Earth, if chosen instead of heaven, will turn out to have been, all along, only a region of hell: and earth, if put second to heaven, to have been from the beginning a part of heaven itself.

The point is not that God will refuse you admission to God's world of eternal happiness if you do not have certain qualities of character: the point is that if people do not have at least the beginnings of those qualities inside them, then no possible external conditions could make a "heaven" for them. If God is Happiness Itself, God's gift of the Holy Spirit poured into our hearts (Rom 5:5) is the beginning of that eternal joy which this world neither gives nor can take from us (John 16:23).

C. S. Lewis affirmed that God designed the human machine to run on Godself.[2] God is the fuel our spirits were designed to burn, or the food our spirits were designed to feed on. There is no other. That is why it is just no good asking God to make us happy in our own way without bothering about God. God cannot give us a happiness and peace apart from Godself, because it is not there. There is no such thing. We welcome Happiness Itself in our eucharistic eating the Body and drinking the Blood of Christ. God—Happiness Itself—is God's own best gift in the Son and the Holy Spirit. Unless God wanted/loved us, we would not be wanting/loving God.

God's love for us is not wearied by our sins, our indifference; and, therefore, it is quite relentless in its determination that we shall be cured of those sins, at whatever cost to us, at whatever cost to God.

Eternal Love is self-giving Love. The Father gives all the Father is and has to the Son. The Son gives himself back to the Father, and gives himself to the world, and for the world to the Father, and thus gives the world in himself back to the Father. God loves us not because we are lovable but because God is Love Itself; not because God needs to receive but because God delights to give. God knows

---

[2] *Mere Christianity,* bk. II, ch. 3, par. 7 (New York: Macmillan, 1958) 54.

how hard we find it to love God above all, and God will be pleased with us as long as we are trying. And God will help us.

Because we love something else more than this world we love this world better than those who know no other. God wants us to love God more, not to love creatures less. We love everything in one way too much (at the expense of our love for God) but in another way we love everything too little. God's works deserve to be loved as God loves them. Our love for God is always all of a piece with the way that we love the persons, places, and things around us. When we have learned to love God better than our earthly dearest, we shall love our earthly dearest better than we do now. True love is always a love for God and creatures as they truly are: God above all, and all else as our limited selves. The joy of true love is lost in loving God for less than what God is, and creatures above all.

To love and admire anything outside ourselves is to take one step away from utter spiritual ruin; though we shall not be well so long as we love and admire anything more than we love and admire God. When we want to be something other than what God wants us to be, we must be wanting what, in fact, will not make us happy. God, as Thomas Aquinas wrote, is Happiness Itself. God gives what God is, not what God is not. God's self-giving love is the gift of Happiness Itself.

To be God, to be like God, and to share God's happiness in creaturely response, to be miserable—these are the only three alternatives. If we will not learn to eat the only food that the universe grows—the only food that any possible universe ever can grow—then we must starve.

The proper good of a creature is self-surrender to its Creator—to enact that relationship which is given in the mere fact of its being a creature. When it does so, it is good and happy. Lest we think this is a hardship, this kind of good originates on a level that infinitely transcends creatures, for Godself, as Son, from all eternity renders back to God as Father by filial love the being which the Father by paternal love eternally generates in the Son. This is the pattern which we were made to reflect—and did reflect in paradise—and wherever the love conferred by the Creator is thus perfectly reciprocated in delighted and delighting communion by the creature, there, most undoubtedly, is heaven, and there the Holy Spirit of Father and Son proceeds.

God knows, loves, and enjoys us in Godself. God does not have to go outside Godself to create, sustain, and fulfill our lives. God knows us in God's truth, loves us in God's goodness, enjoys us in God's beauty. Through the grace and call of the Son and Holy Spirit, the Father wills that we should share the life of the Triune Happiness by becoming truthful in God's truth, good in God's goodness, and lovely in God's beauty. Our eternal happiness is eternal life in communion with Happiness Itself, knowing ourselves in God's truth, loving ourselves in God's goodness, and delighting ourselves in the beauty of God's true goodness. Our God-given destiny is to glorify God by enjoying God forever.

Each of the redeemed shall forever know and praise some one aspect of the divine beauty better than any other creature can. Why else were individuals created, but that God, loving all infinitely, should love each uniquely? God created each person unique. God had a purpose for all these differences. The ins and outs of our individuality are no mystery to God; and one day they will no longer be a mystery to us.

God's knowing and loving and enjoying is the meaning of our creation and existence and destiny. The beauty of God's self-giving wisdom and love and joy calls us to enjoy God above all and in all for our eternal happiness.

# Part II

## BEAUTY IN SCRIPTURE

# 6

# The Look of Love

Gospels are literary-theological units whose structure communicates a theological content. The literary structure of the Synoptic Gospels reveals a relationship between the dynamic of contemplation and the Good News of our redemption. Jesus is the paradigm of the dynamic of divine and human contemplation in salvation history. The Synoptic writers recognize three constants in their accounts of Jesus' saving and transforming contemplation: seeing (vision), saying (word), and doing (action). Jesus' seeing underscores the intrapersonal aspect of his divine and human contemplation. Jesus' speaking underscores the outgoing, interpersonal meaning of the grace and call of his contemplation. Jesus' doing refers to the human transformation that he achieves through his truly meaningful and loving contemplation of the human condition. Jesus' divine and human contemplation, then, is that of a knowing and loving subject with a divine and human interior life that is self-giving in a truly meaningful way for human transformation and fulfillment.

## Jesus' Contemplation as Grace and Call for New Life

Just as God contemplates his first creation in *Genesis,* Jesus contemplates God's new creation in calling his first disciples (Mark 1:16 = Matt 4:18).

> As Jesus passed along the Sea of Galilee, he *saw* Simon and his brother Andrew casting a net into the sea—for they were fishermen. And Jesus *said* to them, *"Follow me and I will make you fish*

> *for people."* And immediately *they* left their nets and *followed him.*

Jesus' contemplation is not that of a remote, indifferent spectator; rather, it expresses the grace and imperative of divine and human love for communion, community, and communications. His contemplation gives new vision, meaning, and life. Simon and Andrew now share Jesus' vision, meaning/purpose, and life as his disciples. Jesus' contemplation enables their communion, community, and communications with him as active participants in his interpersonal/relational life with all divine and human others. Jesus' contemplation gives them Jesus' way of being-together-with-all-others.

## The Contemplative Power of the Risen Christ

The Gospels were written in the light of the risen Christ. Several Synoptic accounts imply the contemplative power of the risen Christ that is operative proleptically in pre-resurrection narratives. The call of Levi (Mark 2:13-14 = Matt 9:9) repeats the vision, word, and action/transformation elements of Jesus' contemplation dynamic; however, it adds a significant new element.

> As he was walking along, he *saw* Levi son of Alphaeus *sitting* at the tax booth, and he *said* to him, "Follow me." And *he got up* and followed him.

Jesus had seen Levi sitting. Levi's change of position suggests something about the transforming impact of the risen Christ enabling Levi to get up/rise up and follow him.

The same idea occurs in the account of Peter's sick mother-in-law (Matt 8:14-15).

> When Jesus entered Peter's house, he *saw* his mother-in-law *lying in bed* with fever; he touched her hand, and the fever left her, and *she got up* and began to serve him.

This account brings out the sacramental character of the risen Christ and his contemplative power to transform human life. Even though Jesus does not speak, his action of touching the sick woman has word-character; actions speak as visible signs of his healing contemplation. The risen Christ frees from the evils that prevent our sharing in his messianic mission of service. The healed woman's rising up to serve Jesus is a visible sign of the just who are even now rising through the power of the risen Christ to share his life/mission.

The triumph of the risen Christ over death is adumbrated in Luke's account of the son of the widow of Nain (7:13-15).

> When the Lord *saw* her, he had *compassion* for her and *said* to her, "Do not weep." Then he came forward and touched the bier, and the bearers stood still. And he *said,* "Young man, I say to you, *rise!*" The dead man *sat up* and began to speak, and Jesus gave him to his mother.

The compassionate contemplation of Jesus expresses the grace and call of the living God to eternal life. The contemplative power of the risen Christ gives *new* life. The former life of the widow's son is finished; his new life has begun in response to the Lord of life. The imperative of the risen Christ to rise, is the imperative of divine love to accept a life that is only Christ's to give.

## Jesus' Contemplative Power of Compassion

The contemplative compassion of Jesus for suffering human-kind finds expression in his call to prayer on their behalf.

> When he *saw* the crowds, he had *compassion* on them, because they were harrassed and helpless, like sheep without a shepherd. Then he *said* to his disciples, "The harvest is plentiful, but the laborers are few; *pray,* therefore, the Lord of the harvest to send out laborers into his harvest."

Jesus calls us to share his contemplative vision and compassion both in prayer and labor for all who suffer. The gift of his Holy Spirit enables us to share his response to human suffering and need. Faith, Lonergan affirmed, is the eye of love which sees what unlove cannot. The contemplative compassion of Jesus liberates us from blindness/unlove toward human misery, drift, hopelessness. "Sheep without a shepherd" expresses the suffering of meaningless, aimless, desperate lives.

## The Contemplation that Instills Faith/Hope

Matthew's account of the woman with hemorrhages (9:22) relates the divine and human contemplation of Jesus to the healing gift of faith/hope.

> Jesus turned, and *seeing* her, he *said,* "Take heart, daughter; your faith has made you well." And instantly the woman *was made well.*

## Jesus' Contemplation Inspires Praise

Prayer is a leading theme of Luke's Gospel. Luke implicitly links prayers of praise with the transforming, healing power of Jesus' contemplation when he recounts the story of the woman who for eighteen years had a spirit which kept her ill. She was stooped over and could not straighten herself up in any way (Luke 13:11).

> When Jesus *saw* her, he *called* her over and *said,* "Woman, you are set free from your ailment." When he laid hands on her, immediately she *stood up straight* and *began praising God.*

The formerly stooped woman now rises to stand straight, reflecting the power of the risen Christ's contemplative compassion and power to transform human life. Praising God for what the risen Christ has done for us is evidence of the new life that we have received. The divine and human compassion of Christ heals and gladdens the grateful heart with the fullness of a new life.

## The Joy of Divine and Human Contemplation

The story of Zacchaeus (Luke 19:1-10) underscores the joy communicated by the transforming contemplation of Jesus.

> When he reached the place, Jesus *looked* up and *said* to him, "Zacchaeus, come down quickly, for today I must stay at your house." And *he came down quickly* and *received him with joy.* When they all saw this, they began to grumble, saying, "He has gone to stay at the house of a sinner." But Zacchaeus *stood* there and said to the Lord, "Behold, half of my possessions, Lord, I shall give to the poor . . ."

Jesus' contemplative love, word, and deed transform human life with a joy that he alone can give. Zacchaeus welcomes the grace and call of the risen Christ to the joy of a new life, a joy that his former wealth had not given him.

## The Contemplative Power of Jesus for Reconciliation

Luke's narrative of Peter's repentance discloses the efficacy of Jesus' contemplative love in reconciliation.

> And the Lord turned and *looked at* Peter; and Peter *remembered the word* of the Lord, how he had *said* to him. . . . He *went out* and *began to weep bitterly.*

The three constants appear in this narrative: Jesus' look of love (contemplation/vision), his word (the meaning of that love), and the transformation that it effects (repentance). Jesus enables us to remember his words, the meaning of his life and love for us, leading us to reconciliation or a change of heart.

## Reciprocity of Divine and Human Contemplation: Prayer

The Synoptic narratives of divine and human contemplation imply that Jesus' contemplation enables ours. The dynamic of loving contemplation revealed in Jesus Christ empowers us to pray, to contemplate, to behold ourselves, all others, the world, and God in the light of the same love with which God beholds/contemplates Godself and all creation within Godself. Luke's account of Jesus and the ten lepers (17:11-16) highlights the four basic aspects of prayer in the context of Jesus' healing contemplation or look/gaze of love.

> Keeping their distance, they called out, saying, "Jesus, Master, have mercy on us!" When he *saw* them, he *said* to them, "Go and show yourselves to the priests." And as they went, *they were made clean.* Then one of them, when he *saw* that *he was healed,* turned back, *praising God* with a loud voice. He prostrated himself at Jesus' feet and thanked him.

The four basic elements of prayer (petition, praise, worship, thanksgiving) are rendered possible by Jesus' transforming look/gaze of love (contemplation). The story brings out the human freedom to reciprocate. Although God/Jesus contemplates/beholds all with love, only a few reciprocate. God loves all, independently of a response in kind.

## Scriptural Iconography for Contemplation and Action

Three dimensions of Jesus' transfiguring contemplation of humankind: loving gaze (vision), speaking (meaningful word), transfiguring action (deed).

| Text | Vision | Word | Transformation |
|---|---|---|---|
| Luke 7:13-15 | And when the Lord **saw** her, he had compassion on her, "Do not weep." | And he **said,** "Young man, I say to you, arise." | And the dead man **sat up,** and began to speak. |
| Matt 9:9 | As Jesus passed on from there, he **saw** a man called Mt. sitting at the tax office. | and he **said** to him "Follow me." | And he **rose** and followed him. |
| Matt 8:14-15 | And when Jesus entered Peter's house, he **saw** his mother-in-law sick with fever. | he **touched** her hand, and the fever left her. | and she **rose** and served him. |
| Matt 4:18-20 | As he walked by the sea of Galilee, he **saw** two brothers . . . | And he **said** to them, "Follow me and I will make you fishers of men." | Immediately they left their nets and **followed** him. |
| Matt 9:36-38 | When he **saw** the crowds, he had **compassion** for them, because they were harassed and helpless, like sheep without a shepherd. | Then he **said** to his disciples, "The harvest is plentiful, but the laborers are few: | **pray** therefore the Lord of the harvest to send laborers into his harvest." |
| Matt 9:22 | Jesus turned, and **seeing** her | he **said,** "Take heart, daughter; your faith has made you well." | And instantly the woman was **made well.** |

| | | | |
|---|---|---|---|
| Luke 13:11-13 | And there was a woman who . . . was bent over and could not fully straight herself. And when he **saw** her, | he called her and **said** to her, "Woman, you are freed from your infirmity." And he laid his hand upon her, | and immediately she was **made straight,** and she **praised** God. |
| Luke 17:11-16 | . . . "Jesus, Master, have mercy on us." When he **saw** them | he **said** to them, "Go and show yourselves to the priests." And as they went they were cleansed. | Then one of them . . . turned back, **praising** God with a loud voice; and he fell on his face at Jesus' feet, **giving him thanks.** |
| Luke 22:61-2 | And the Lord turned and **looked** at Peter. | And Peter **remembered** the word of the Lord, how he had **said** to him . . . | And he went out and **wept bitterly.** |
| Luke 19:1-10 | . . . And there was a man named Zacchaeus . . . And he sought to see who Jesus was, but could not. . . . And when Jesus came to the place, he **looked up** | and **said** to him, "Zacchaeus, make haste and come down . . . | So he made haste and came down, and **received him joyfully.** |

# 7

# The "Beautiful" Shepherd

John's description of Jesus as the Good Shepherd has a relevance for the theology of beauty that derives from the Old Testament notion of God as shepherd. The people of Israel are of
shepherd origins. Abraham was rich in cattle (Gen 13:2); Isaac
possessed flocks and herds (26:14); Jacob, who married Rachel,
the shepherdess, is presented in Genesis as an ideal shepherd and
is remembered by Israel as such (Jdt 8:26). He is described as the
caring, loving and self-giving shepherd (Gen 33:13-14). Even
Joseph is described as a shepherd, together with his brothers
(37:2). Moses is remembered as shepherd of Israel (Exod 3:1; Isa
63:11; Num 27:17; Ps 77:19-20). David is also presented as a
shepherd before being elected king of Israel (1 Sam 16:11). Even
here, as in the case of Jacob, David is depicted giving an account
of himself as a courageous, self-giving shepherd before King Saul
(1 Sam 17:34-36).

The supreme shepherd of Israel is Godself. Moses and David
are only his representatives. It is God who has led the people of
Israel out of Egypt and has given them a place of rest where they
can dwell in safety. God delegates to David the function of shep-
herding his people Israel (2 Sam 7). God remains the owner of
the flock. The shepherd image of God is embedded in the living
piety of Israel. God is directly called a shepherd in four places in
the Old Testament (Gen 48:15; 49:24; Pss 23:1; 80:2). All these
contexts emphasize the care and concern which God shows for
Israel.

The Old Testament classifies the activities of God as shepherd in six distinct, basic roles. These roles are interdependent and, in some ways, include each other: leading/guiding (Ps 80:2; Deut 29:4; Exod 15:13; Isa 49:9); feeding/sustaining (Ps 23:1; Isa 49:9; Jer 50:19; Ezek 34:13-14); guarding/protecting/assuring (Jer 31:10; Exod 12:42; Ezek 34:30; Ps 121:3-8); gathering/searching/delivering/judging (Jer 23:3; Mic 2:12; Ezek 34:11-13; Ps 28:9; Zech 9:16); caring/comforting/healing (Zech 10:3; Exod 15:26; Isa 57:18-19; Jer 17:14; Ezek 34:15; Ps 23:4; Deut 1:31); knowing/attending/bonding with/alliance (Jer 23:1-3; Ezek 34:6, 25-31; Zech 13:7-9).

The Old Testament writers depict God as a shepherd who acts in favor of God's people. God is involved in the life of God's people. God is with them, whatever the circumstances, so they can be secure. God gathers, binds, and strengthens them.

In John's Gospel Jesus affirms "I am the good shepherd. The good shepherd lays down his life for his sheep" (10:11). Although John presents Jesus as the shepherd of the flock, he does not prescind from the Old Testament tradition that God the Father is the sole proprietor of the flock. The Father has given the sheep to Jesus that he might accomplish his saving work in them (10:29). As no one will be able to snatch them from Jesus, so no one will be able to snatch them from the Father (10:28-29).

John, as the Synoptics, takes up the Old Testament tradition of the image of the shepherd to show that Jesus fulfills the eschatological prophecies. In Jesus, the traditional biblical theme of God as Shepherd is affirmed to be both renewed and fulfilled beyond all expectations. Jesus, the eternal Word, possessed life from all eternity (1:4), which he has received from the Father (5:26) and gives it in abundance (10:10) to all those his Father has given him" (17:2). He himself is the life (11:25; 14:6) and "the light of life (8:12). Whoever receives and obeys the commandment of Jesus, which he received from the Father, will have eternal life (12:47-50). This is to say that life in John means also complete communion with Jesus, the Good Shepherd, whose death and resurrection is the laying down or communication of that life for his sheep. The self-giving life and love of Jesus, the Good Shepherd, is the same that he receives from his Father, the Shepherd of Israel.

Significantly, when John affirms that Jesus is the Good Shepherd, the Greek adjective that he uses to qualify shepherd is *kalos*. The basic meaning of this epithet is "fit," "healthy," or "useful." *Kalos* also means "attractive," "lovely," or "pleasant." Finally, it can be applied to the inward disposition or spirit of a person. Here it means "morally good" or "beautiful" as a human being. It refers to one's inner beauty as it shows itself in outward form. Jesus not only fulfills the idea of the authentic shepherd, but he also fulfills the idea of that shepherd's attractive loveliness. His inner beauty/excellence/goodness is outwardly manifested and perceived. It is the beauty/goodness of his person that will "draw all persons to himself" (12:32). And this beauty of his goodness is supremely seen in the act by which he would so draw them, wherein he lays down his life for his sheep.

Jesus, in the fulfillment of his saving work as the messianic Shepherd, implies the intimate relationship between the shepherd and his sheep. The goodness/beauty of the shepherd cannot be understood without reference to the sheep that he loves, guides, sustains, and defends. The compelling beauty of his self-giving love and goodness saves the world.

John uses the word *kalos* four other times in his gospel: twice in 2:10 in reference to the water that Jesus changed into wine at the wedding feast of Cana and twice in 10:32-33 in reference to the works of Jesus. This word, in John's Gospel, is applied uniquely to Jesus or to his mission. It affirms the supreme excellence and uniqueness of Jesus as the shepherd of the new people of God, fulfilling in himself and going beyond all the former Old Testament prototypes as their messianic fulfillment. He came "not to condemn the world, but that the world might be saved through him" (3:17). He came "that they may have life, and have it abundantly" (10:10), by laying down his life for his sheep. Jesus gives his life "to gather into one the children of God who are scattered abroad" (11:52). As the Good Shepherd he must bring together the scattered sheep (10:16). Jesus on the cross becomes the unifying reality to whom all will be drawn (12:32); the saving beauty of his self-giving love overcomes our alienation from God and from one another.

The beauty of Jesus the shepherd, who lays down his life, is the model of life for his flock. As he who loves to the end (13:1) gives his life for us, so should we be so united in Jesus' love as to be able to give our life for one another. As the sheep of his flock we are called to follow and to share the self-giving life of the one shepherd. Jesus' constant availability to give his life for others, although culminating on the cross, began from the moment of his incarnation. The final definitive self-surrender of his life had its beginnings when the Word became flesh (1:14). It is the beautiful sign of the greatest love which the Lord has for us and which we should have for one another (15:13; 1 John 3:16). It clarifies what it means to be good/beautiful *(kalos)*.

The narrative of the Good Shepherd reminds us that love must be perceived. If God wishes to make God's love for the world known, it must be recognizable—in spite of, and because of, its being totally other. Love is really only perceived by love. We must have some notion of love if we are to understand the unselfish love of someone who loves us and not regard it as something we can make use of. Similarly, an art critic must have an innate or acquired flair for the qualities of a great work of art in order to distinguish it from mediocre forms. This preparation of the individual by which he or she is placed on the level of the thing revealed and attuned to it, is, for an individual, that habit of mind (which may be called the trinity of faith, love, and hope) which must be present, at least in embryo, for a true encounter—and, moreover, can be present, because God's love, which is always grace, bears with it and communicates the necessary conditions for being recognized.

Urs von Balthasar explains the enabling power of God's love in terms of a mother whose love evokes the love of her child.[1]

> After a mother has smiled for some time at her child, it will begin to smile back; she has awakened love in its heart, and in waking

---

[1] Urs von Balthasar, *Love Alone,* trans. A. Dru (New York: Herder and Herder, 1963) 61–2.

the child to love, she awakes also recognition. The sense impressions, at first empty of meaning, gather meaningfully round the "thou"; the whole apparatus of knowledge and understanding comes into play with its power to perceive and to conceive because the play of love has been started by the child's mother. In the same way, God explains himself before man as love. Love radiates from God and instills the light of love in the heart of man: precisely a light in which he can perceive this—absolute—love. "For God, who commanded the light to shine out of the darkness, has shined in our hearts, whose shining is to kindle in us the knowledge of the Glory of God in the face of Jesus Christ" (2 Cor 4:6). The very ground of being smiles upon us in the face of Christ, as a father or mother might smile at us. We are his creatures and so a seed of love, God's image, lies dormant within us. But just as no child can awaken to love until it is loved, no human heart can come to the knowledge of God without the free gift of his grace, in the image of his Son.

# 8

# Scriptural Icons

The Church employs its Scriptures for the attainment of human authenticity in Christian conversion, conceived as both event and lifelong process. Its pedagogy aims at the transformation of the cognitive and affective consciousness of human *subjects,* of the decision-making and activity of responsible human *agents,* in every sphere of their *relational existence* (intrapersonal, interpersonal, social, national, international). The theocentric and Christocentric process of self-transcendence in Christian conversion entails four complementary aspects: *metanoia* (transformation), *kenosis* (generosity), *diakonia* (service), and *koinonia* (friendship).

Scripture is both informative and above all transformative. The Old Testament is a call to theocentric self-transcendence in religious conversion. The New Testament is a call to Christocentric self-transcendence in Christian conversion. Christocentricity guarantees the authenticity of theocentricity in religious conversion.

Conversion entails the transformation of the human and its world in all the spheres of human intentionality and conscious operations. As *subjects,* our cognitive and affective consciousness undergoes a transformation in both the event and continuous process of conversion. The transformed or 'converted' subject has a new way of knowing and loving: it is no longer the center of its world. The theocentric self-transcendence of religious conversion becomes Christocentric when we are enabled by Jesus Christ to know as we are known and to love as we are loved (1 Cor 13:12; 1 John 3:2; Gal 4:9). The theocentric self-transcendence of Jesus Christ enables our own; it transforms our cognitive and affective consciousness by making us sons in the Son.

Conversion entails the transformation of our lives as *agents,* responsible for decisions and actions. Conversion means a new way of deciding and acting in the light of our new way of knowing and loving, transformed by the grace and call of Jesus Christ for accepting new responsibilities. We no longer live for ourselves as our own little gods in a state of self-idolatry, but *for* God, accepting responsibility before God for our decisions and actions.

Conversion entails the transformation of every sphere of our relational existence: the intrapersonal world of our interior life, the interpersonal world of our family and friends, the social world of our educational, political, recreational, and other communities, the national and international worlds. Our transformed consciousness influences our decision and action in every sphere of our relational existence. We are summoned by the grace and demand of God to act responsibly in every sphere or context of our relational existence. To love God means accepting responsibility *to* God, seeking to learn and to do God's will, in all our relational existence.

Scripture serves the pedagogy of the Church both for *ascertaining* and *promoting* the authenticity of Christian life. The Church attributes *canonicity* to its sacred writings because it deems them normative for ascertaining and fostering an authentically theocentric life in communion with the body of Christ and the temple of his Spirit. Scripture is affirmed to be the word of God's truth and love which invites us to share in God's freedom to love all as truly as God does (John 15:15). Scripture is the divinely inspired pedagogy of the Church which serves to free us from the obstacles to that divine and universal love which is the transcendent destiny and fulfillment of all humankind.

Scripture promotes human freedom and authenticity in Christian conversion. Four New Testament concepts express four complementary aspects of this liberating event and lifelong process. *Metanoia,* the transformation of our cognitive and affective consciousness or interior life, the source of decision and action in every sphere of our relational existence, implies that liberation

from selfishness which enables us to share Jesus Christ's universal love and wisdom. *Kenosis,* the self-giving generosity of Jesus
Christ, frees us to invest our lives in others in his Spirit. *Diakonia,*
the self-giving that, devoid of self-interest, frees us to collaborate
with Jesus Christ in making a genuine contribution to others.
*Koinonia,* the culmination of the conversion process, is our communion in the communion of the Three Persons. The friendship,
reciprocity, peace, and community of the friends of God is the
sacrament of the Eternal Love/Life that unites the Father, the Son,
and the Spirit. *Koinonia* is impossible without *metanoia, kenosis,*
and *diakonia.* The self-giving of the triune God enables these four
aspects of our self-giving (see Acts 2:42-48). The self-giving
Father is known in the self-giving of the body of Christ and the
temple of the Spirit. Christian conversion occurs wherever we are
becoming community/covenant persons, giving our lives for others in the Spirit of Jesus and his Father. Scripture as God's word
is a call to conversion, and that is always a call to communion or
friendship with God and all others.

## Scriptural Iconography for Christian Conversion

The community of faith employs its scriptural iconography as
a matrix for Christian conversion. Believing, hoping, loving,
deciding—all are fundamental activities at the heart of all human
life. These activities involve human motivation. Vision is essential to human life, inasmuch as it is an orientation to decision
and action. We cannot do what we cannot, at least in some way,
imagine or envisage. In Johannine theology no one can come to
Christ unless the Father draws him (6:44). Christ is the icon, the
image through which the Father transforms each particular
human life story. In the measure that our image/vision of Christ
is in or out of focus, is more or less oblique, in that measure will
we reflect explicitly or implicitly what is authentically human
and divine. Our lives bear witness to a basic vision; this vision
includes images of ourselves, others, the world, human integrity
and failure, God, and so on. However unclear, distorted, or false
our vision (or images), there is no human life story without it.
Vision, including all the images associated with it, is integral to

human motivation and action; it shapes our lives. Truly good lives imply true vision.

The life story, the humanity of Jesus, is the icon disclosing his God and Father to the world. To see him is to see the Father (John 12:45; 14:9). The life story of the crucified and risen Jesus is the paradigmatic image for Christian faith. Through its scriptural iconography, the community of faith calls us to communicate the likeness of God by sharing the likeness of Jesus in whom God is rendered visible, authentically imaginable, and imitable as our way, our truth, and our life. Inasmuch as we cannot do what we can in no way imagine, Jesus, as the perfect icon of God, motivates faith to a new way of being-in-the-world-together-with-all-others. Inasmuch as motivation is commensurate with the concreteness and vividness and beauty of an image, the life story of the crucified and risen Jesus has proved a historically compelling image of God that has radically transformed the lives of millions through the centuries. It corrects, transforms, and educates our vision of God.

The biblical pedagogy of the Church, its scriptural iconography, recognizes that an authentic image of ourselves, others, and the world implies an authentic image of God—the pure of heart shall see God, because they "see" God as God really is in relation to the complexity of their lives as beings-in-the-world-with-others. A distorted image of self implies a distorted image of God.

The life story of Jesus and his parables reveal the coherence of his images of faith. They reveal his interpretation of life: his own life, the external life he encountered in the lives of others and himself. Christian conversion is the process by which the life of Jesus, the story told by his life, so transforms our cognitive-affective core that our life stories become icons of the same God as his.

The parable of the Talents (Matt 25:14-30; cf. Mark 13:34; Luke 19:11-27) throws light upon the coherence of our motivating images and the need for their transformation in response to the challenge of the Good News. The unproductive life of the wicked and lazy servant is explained in terms of fear—he believes his master to be a "hard man." His image of his master engenders fear and distrust that, in turn, render the servant's life unproductive both for himself and for others. Failure to live with a true image of the master precludes sharing in his happiness. Without a basic trust in, and gratitude to his generous master, the servant abandons himself in vain to his own plan for being safe. Without what we might call a eucharistic disposition, the image of God disclosed by our life story will be at variance with the image we explicitly attempt to project in our prayers, our hymns, and our telling of the gospel story.

The scriptural iconography of each evangelist enables us to see complementary aspects of God and God's love in Jesus Christ. *Mark* sees in the suffering Messiah and Servant of God (10:45) the face of a loving God serving all humankind, giving his life for all. The self-abandonment of the crucified is the self-gift of God for all. *Matthew* affirms that Christ is Emmanuel, God-with-us, the Messiah Son of God in whom God is present among God's people (1:23). His Gospel of the Church affirms that God abides with God's people in the person of Jesus, who is acting in their fellowship (28:20). If God is love, Matthew sees God's face in the brothers and sisters of Jesus. *Luke* stresses the outgoing and universal compassion of God in Jesus Christ's concern for outcasts, sinners, Samaritans, and the poor. Luke sees the face of God in the universal outreach and compassion of Jesus, an all-embracing love without limits. *John* affirms that in Jesus Christ we share in the life of the triune communion. The mutual indwelling of Father and Son is communicated in the gift of their Spirit (14:15-16). John sees in Jesus Christ and his community of faith the indwelling community that is the eternal life and love of the Blessed Trinity. The indwelling love of the Three Persons for one another is manifest in the outgoing love of Jesus Christ and his community of faith. John sees in the reciprocal love of Christians both the indwelling and outgoing love of the Three Persons as the origin and ground and destiny or fulfillment of all humankind. The Church is the sacrament/icon of the triune communion, the efficacious sign of the eternal love even now transforming human relationships into relationships of a friendship/love that not even death itself can terminate. The joy of that friendship/love is one that this world cannot take from us because it is not this world's to give. The Good News of what John sees in Jesus Christ is that the eternal friendship/love is both God's and God's will/destiny for us. The divine will for us is always the divine love for us.

The scriptural iconography of the evangelists implies that seeing God in Jesus Christ means seeing the whole Jesus Christ in the fullness of his interpersonal life: together with his brothers and sisters, no less than with his Father and Spirit. Whoever lives by the same life-principle is a part of his interpersonal life: "For whoever does the will of my Father in heaven is my brother, and sister, and mother" (Matt 12:50). The interpersonal life of Jesus Christ is the matrix for the Christian vision of an interpersonal God in the triune communion of eternal love. The self-giving and sharing that is Jesus Christ's interpersonal life enables our vision/ seeing/image of the self-giving and sharing Three Persons, creating and sustaining and drawing all human life to fulfillment within the triune communion. The Gospels symbolize the unrestricted nature of the triune God's love to which all humankind is constitutively oriented by presenting Jesus as God's revealing image, summoning us to communion in that love. The mystery of that love for us seen/imaged/envisioned in Jesus Christ generates the faith, hope, and love in both the event and lifelong process of Christian conversion. Such conversion means faith in the reality of God's self-giving love *seen* in Jesus Christ. Although the wisdom of the world deems the self-giving life and death of Jesus foolishness, the converted subject finds in the Cross and resurrection both the strength to reject that wisdom and the firm hope that his or her self-giving will not prove futile. The authenticity of our response to Jesus' injunction to love God above all finds its verification in the decisions and actions by which we follow Jesus in costly self-giving love for the neighbor both within and outside the Christian community.

The revolutionary image of God in the crucified Christ identifies God as a participant in human suffering and death, willingly sharing the extremes of human limitation with a love that liberates us from all we most dread. Islam, in contrast, cannot imagine such a God who would allow a true prophet like Jesus to undergo public disgrace, atrocious suffering, and death. For Islam, therefore, the death of Jesus is a mere illusion created by an angel that takes his place at Allah's behest. Buddhists, similarly, cannot imagine Ultimate Reality choosing to participate in a condition that their religion seeks to avoid. The Greeks, for whose gods the human condition of suffering and death was little more than a spectator sport, were equally unable to entertain such an image of God. Although the Hindus are able to accept the notion of incarnated gods, their gods avoid the punishments for evil that are suffering and death. For the Jews (and other religions) the notion of God incarnate is sufficiently blasphemous, to say nothing of their God participating in human suffering and death! The perfect image of God in the crucified and risen Jesus is at the heart of the Christian community's scriptural iconography and pedagogy for confronting the problem of evil in all its bewildering forms. Suffering, evil, and death cannot overcome the invincible love of the crucified and risen Christ in whose face the Christian community sees its God and proclaims that God is Love (1 John 4:7 and following). The Christian community's vision of God in the crucified and risen Christ unites it in the conviction that the Spirit of the Son's invincible love given to us (Gal 4:6) will prevail over the powers of darkness and can achieve something of Christ's heroism in all of us, empowering us to meet the demands of that love in all the spheres of our relational life.

Jesus is the human image of the divine love at the service of all humankind. When he takes the role of the servant washing the feet of his disciples, he tells them that his role is paradigmatic of their own relationship to one another and to the kingdom (John 13:14-15). His service is the sign/image of his living in the Spirit that is both his life/love given to the Father and his Father's life/love given to him. His service is in giving to all the Spirit that unites Father and Son in mutual indwelling love. The kingdom of God is coming where we welcome and serve each other in that same Spirit. The final words of this Last Supper scene are Jesus' call to sharing his service: "If you know these things, blessed are you if you do them" (John 13:17). Conversion means living in that Spirit that is transforming our lives with the love that is the life of both Father and Son.

Mark's scriptural iconography is a literary and theological unit whose structure discloses the integrating center of Jesus' life in two ways that are normative for Christian conversion.

Jesus lives for divine rather than human approval. Mark structures his narrative to indicate that Jesus lives for God above all.

Jesus' unpopularity is commensurate to the progress that he makes in fulfilling his Father's will. The hostility that Jesus encounters intensifies as the sphere of his activity expands. Religious leaders clash with him and decide that he must die (2:1–3:6). His family and relatives reject him (6:1-6). His disciples oppose him (8:32). The crowds turn against him (14:43; 15:14). The military mock him (15:16-20) after he has been condemned to death by the civil authorities (15:15). Disciples, friends, and family abandon him at Golgotha where some women are described as observing events "from a distance" (15:40). Jesus dies alone. His life story culminates in obedience to his Father's will. He enjoys no human solidarity or affirmation, but only mockery and contempt. The meaning is not clear of both his rebuke to Peter for thinking the way of men rather than of God (8:33) and of his affirmation that God alone is good (10:18).

Jesus lives to share his interior life with all humankind. Mark makes this clear by structuring his narrative around three authentic and full affirmations of Jesus' identity in which he implies that only the Lover (Father) authentically and adequately recognizes and knows the Beloved (Son). At the beginning (1:11) and during (9:7) the life story of Jesus, the Lover explicitly identifies Jesus as the Beloved. Only through the death of Jesus for "the many" (10:45; 14:24) is the Gentile centurion, the archetype of the many, able to share the Lover's recognition of the Beloved. These three affirmations of Jesus' divine Sonship make up the beginning, the middle, and the completion of Jesus' life story. Jesus is fully aware of his God-given meaning and value, mission and purpose from the beginning to the completion of his life story. Aware of the Lover who has called him Beloved, Jesus is enabled to transmit to the "many," symbolized by the Gentile centurion, the transforming and saving reality of that love. If the baptismal narrative reveals Jesus as the person whose very existence is that of being loved by God, the Transfiguration narrative reveals that love as constituting Jesus as the sacrament of God's love for all humankind. The transfigured humanity of Jesus is the outward and visible sign of the inward: an invisible favor that infallibly brings about that which it declares. Mark would not be writing the story of the Beloved Christ if he and his hearers had not already heard the voice that calls them "my Beloved." Mark is writing the story of the One who is the supreme Symbol (sacramental sign) of the Lover-Beloved relationship, the efficacious Symbol *(signum efficax)* that draws together *(symbollein)* all humankind to become what they contemplate.

Every life story requires an initiating vision; so the Marcan Jesus sees the meaning of his life's story in the moment he starts to tell it. Jesus' life and mission begin with the major statement of the vision from which all else springs. Mark presents Jesus' knowledge and vision of his own beloved Sonship as the energizing source and dynamic principle that binds the disparate elements of his life story together. We can in no way do what we cannot envision. The baptismal affirmation of Jesus as the Beloved Son of God gives Jesus the vision of who he is and what his story should tell. Mark structures his story so that the vision that initiates the life of Jesus is present throughout his entire life story. The appreciative voice of the Father is heard by Jesus throughout the length of his saving mission. It defines Jesus as one who at core is in relation to the Father; it defines the character of the favor and authority he enjoys from heaven. The baptismal account seems to imply that it was Jesus alone who heard the voice; the voice testifies to the ontological basis of Jesus' ability to communicate the concrete goodness of being loved by God. It is because Jesus is the unique Beloved of God that he can make us beloved. It is from this that all else flows.

At the Transfiguration, the heavenly voice comes almost as a response to Peter's exclamation. Peter and heaven are represented as speaking. At the Transfiguration the representatives of the new People of God share the vision and hear the voice. Jesus is represented as transforming; the Beloved is making us beloved. The Transfigured transfigures. At the Transfiguration a command is added to the words heard at the baptism: ". . . listen to him." The Lover not only loves the Beloved but also demands that others listen to the Beloved. The Lover's authority is invested in the Beloved. It is witnessed by the Gentile centurion who stands for the many for whom Christ's blood was poured out (14:24). "Truly," he declares, "was this man the Son of God" (15:39). This confession of faith represents for Mark a full confession of the

Easter faith of his readers in the divinity of the crucified and risen Son of God.

The three affirmations of Sonship suggest a Markan model for the entire event and process of Christian conversion. The relationship of human persons to the Beloved Son moves from nonrecognition (baptism) through incipient recognition (Transfiguration) to full recognition (Golgotha). Mark's readers will experience the goodness of God's affirming love in their lives only as they allow themselves to be drawn to him along the Way of the Cross. In the self-gift of the Son, God wills to make us the locus of God's own self-giving to all humanity. In the measure that we allow ourselves to be totally receptive to God, in that measure can God make us the fountain from which this love will flow to our brothers and sisters.

Mark's scriptural iconography is an extended symbol of God's self-investment in the Son, the Beloved, a self-investing love that calls forth and creates love in all who receive the Spirit of the Son. Mark's Gospel summons each reader to bear the words of God: "You are my Son, the Beloved. My favor rests on you." Mark is engaged in the cognitive-affective transformation of his readers, a transformation that issues from the felt-meaning of God's loving self-investment in their lives. Mark wants his readers to accept as the integrating center of their lives the Supreme and Beloved Goodness whose life has been poured out for them. Letting God be God means letting God invest in our lives the fulfilling goodness of the Beloved Son and Spirit.

## Conversion as Remembering

The psalmist believed that the dead inhabit the land of oblivion (88:13); they are in a state of spiritual amnesia. God no longer works wonders for the dead (88:11). They cannot remember God because their relationship with God has been severed. Sadness reigns in the world of the dead (Deut 34:8). The joyless state of the dead derives from their inability to remember God. They do not share in the joy of Israel's worship and praise of God (Ps 88:11; Isa 38:18). The psalmist assumes that only where death reigns is there no praise of or joy in God; where there is life, there is praise and joy.

The Church's biblical pedagogy is grounded in the divine and human remembering that is one of the forms that God's creative and transforming *love* takes. God's remembering this people is God's loving/preserving/saving them. We exist and survive because God remembers us. God's remembering is God's *self-giving,* always a gift *(gratia operans),* a divine initiative enabling our reciprocity *(gratia operans)* in self-giving remembering or communion with God. This remembering is one of the forms that God's *freedom* takes in securing both our freedom *from* oblivion/alienation and our freedom *for* fulfillment in communion with God. No one forces God to remember, to love, or to care for us. God's remembering is always God's self-giving *call to communion* or *reciprocity,* enabling our *responsibility.* God reminds us to remember God; God calls us to recall God. God's remembering/loving is universal. God remembers/loves all humankind without exception. God's remembering/loving is the common good of the universe, the source and ground and fulfillment of all humankind. The unity of all in a "universe" is rooted in God's remembering all together, loving all with this all-encompassing love, the common good in which all created goodness participates for its existence, development, and fulfillment. (Luke implies that God's love forgets nothing when he has Jesus recount three stories in chapter 15—of persons seeking what they have lost. "Jesus, remember me when you come into your kingdom" (Luke 23:42), the words of the Good Thief, also imply the loving/saving remembering of a God who forgets no one.)

Prayer, worship, liturgy—all are forms of theocentric self-transcendence in remembering God. Prayers of gratitude and thanksgiving express our remembering God's gifts. Prayers of petition are ways of remembering God's loving concern for our welfare. All true prayer expresses our remembering that God remembers/loves us, implicitly affirming that God is good.

Our remembering God in the cognitive and affective self-transcending activity of prayer is, even now, an experience of our ultimate meaning, perfection, and destiny/future. We are most fully ourselves when we are in prayerful communion with our divine Origin-Ground-Destiny. As relational beings, we most experience absurdity, meaninglessness, and frustration when we are out of touch with or oblivious to Ultimate Reality/God. Our remembering God is implicitly our experience of God's remembering us; for our prayer is always a response to God who is reminding us that God is our Creator-Sustainer-Fulfillment. The Spirit of God is where it is actively reminding us to remember "Abba, Father"; for God sends the Spirit of the Son into our hearts for this purpose (Gal 4:6).

God has given us the Spirit of the Son to do what we could not otherwise do: "He will teach you everything and remind you of all that I have said to you" (John 14:26). Jesus' gift of the Spirit reminds us to forgive others and calls us to be reconciled with them (John 20:22). God's gift of the Spirit of the Son transforms human life, making all things new (e.g., John 1:30; Matt 3:16; God reintegrates our lives through this Spirit of reconciliation which enables us to do what would otherwise be impossible. God alone actually loves all persons. Apart from the gift of God's Spirit, it is humanly impossible to love all persons, especially our enemies. Peacemakers remind us of and recall us to the Spirit of God which renews and reintegrates all human life in Christ. The Lord's Prayer teaches us that we cannot know Our Father in the biblical sense of an intimate personal relationship apart from our willingness to be reconciled with all others. Our liturgical remembering both expresses and forms our identity in the triune communion where we learn to forgive others as God forgives us. It reminds us who we truly are and calls us to our real selves in the triune communion with all others.

Amnesia is an illness that involves an identity crisis. Individuals forget their past, their story, their relationships. Inasmuch as individuals are interpersonal and relational realities, amnesia deprives them of their identity. They forget who they are in the fullness of their interpersonal and social reality. Amnesia is, therefore, a form of personal disintegration in which persons lose or "forget" themselves. Amnesia threatens communities and societies as well; for they can forget their story, their tradition, their identity. The liturgy of both Israel and the Church is a form of remembering that both unites and preserves the community of faith. To forget their story of God, their common heritage, would entail their destruction as a people. Recounting the wonderful deeds of God for God's people, Moses warns his people never to forget them

(Deut 6:10-13). Remembering is the law of survival: "Remember how Yahweh your God" (Deut 8:2); "Be sure that if you forget Yahweh your God . . . you will most certainly perish" (Deut 8:19). The Lord's Supper entails the same liturgical imperative of remembering for the life of the Church: "Do this in memory of me" (Luke 22:19; 1 Cor 11:24 and following).

The leaders and priests of both Israel and the Church must be able to remind their people to preserve them; they must know their story/tradition or spiritual heritage to communicate it in liturgy, evangelization, ministries, and other forms of witness. Leaders and priests function as reminders of the people, recalling the story and its meaning in Scripture and tradition, proclaiming and manifesting its true goodness for all both in word and deed. Liturgical, catechetical, and evangelical reminding is the task of priests as leaders of the ecclesial community. As servants of the poor in society, they remind the people of the mission of Jesus; they recall them to share in his life of service for the reintegration and salvation of all.

God reminds and recalls this people through the gift of the Son and the Spirit. God's reminding and recalling constitute the covenant community as a reminding and recalling community of faith with a mission of communicating the good news of God's love for all. The body of Christ and the temple of his Spirit, the sacrament of the triune communion, reminds all of the Father's love and calls all to welcome it. The Church is the sacrament of the re-membering and reminding Trinity. Its members participate in the priesthood of its remembering and reminding Lord, proclaiming and manifesting the true goodness of the triune communion as the origin and ground and perfection of all human life.

God has identified us with Godself through the Son and the Spirit. God reminds us of our God-given identity and calls us to welcome it through and within the body of the Son and the temple of the Spirit, saving us from anonymity/spiritual amnesia for the discovery of our real selves in the triune communion. The Spirit of the Father and Son has been given to us to remind us of our God-given identity (John 14:26). Father and Son remember us and call/remind us to welcome our God-given identity in their gift of the Spirit. Idolatry, the apotheosis of created realities in the

service of a human self-apotheosis, is always a rejection of our
God-given identity within the triune communion. It is a form of
spiritual amnesia or oblivion with regard to our true identity or
real selves. Idolatry is the futile attempt to give ourselves an identity other than our real and God-given identity; Scripture and
tradition are the Church's response to the grace of God's remembering and the demand of God's reminding. They express the collective wisdom of the remembering community of faith in both
the event and lifelong process of becoming the friends of God.
The collective wisdom of Scripture and tradition serves as a matrix for cultivating and educating the faith and hope and love of
the divinely remembered and reminded people of God. The community of faith employs the resources of its collective wisdom for
discerning the grace and demand of God for its maturation and
fulfillment. God's gifts entail responsibilities to be discerned and
met in the light of the Church's wisdom tradition.

Scripture and tradition assure us that God is faithful to God's
promises. God remembers these promises or commitments. God is
reliable, trustworthy, responsible. Love, divine and human, means
remembering our promises, commitments, responsibilities, vows.
Human existence, development, and fulfillment evidence God's
remembering these promises, commitments. Authentically personal
life, divine and human, entails the keeping of promises and commitments. The pedagogy of the community of faith in the service
of Christian conversion teaches us that to become the friends of
God, living in God's love, we must share God's trustworthiness,
reliability, and fidelity. The community of faith teaches us to pray
for the Spirit of the Father and the Son in whose love we can overcome our proclivity to irresponsibility, untrustworthiness, infi-
delity, and aimlessness. That same community teaches that the
Cross represents the communion of divine and human remember-
ing/love in accepting costly commitment and responsibility.
Christian conversion is always a call to communion, community,
and friendship—divine and human—based on commitment, fidelity, the ability or will to keep our promises. Communion, community, and friendship disintegrate with our refusal to endure the
limitations of others who do not fully gratify, support, or console
us. The self-giving Spirit of the Father's patient love is revealed

in God's crucified Son's costly commitment to human fulfillment in the triune communion.

God remembers/loves and reminds/calls us in God's word and image, Jesus Christ. The remembered/beloved and reminded/called community of faith has been called into existence and is sustained in its existence and development by that same word and image. Jesus Christ is the living word and image/embodiment of the Good News, the sign of the kingdom, manifesting what human beings are like when they are under the rule of God. Similarly, God's body, the Church, is the living word and image of the Good News, the sign of the kingdom, God's new society manifesting, however imperfectly, what the human community is like when it comes under the rule of God. The Good News of God's loving purpose for all humankind is manifested and proclaimed in Jesus Christ and his body, the Church, where the Word of God becomes visible and the image of God becomes audible. God has manifested/imaged and proclaimed Godself by sending the only Son: "No one has ever seen God, but God the only Son . . . has made him known" (John 1:18). So Jesus could say: "He who has seen me has seen the Father" (John 14:9); and Paul could add that Jesus is "the image of the invisible God" (Col 1:15). Similarly, the invisible God who was made visible in Jesus Christ continues to manifest/image this very self in Christians when they love one another: "No one has ever seen God, but if we love each other, God lives in us and God's love is made perfect in us" (1 John 4:12). To the extent that the body of Christ is transformed into a community of love grounded in truth, God visibly and audibly substantiates the credibility of this Good News for all, opening the eyes of the blind and unstopping the ears of the deaf for the transformation of all humankind into a truthful and loving community.

The eucharistic community of faith thanks God for the gift of its life in the remembering Spirit of God's word and image, Jesus Christ, the epitome of all communion between God and humankind. God's self-giving enables the eucharistic community to believe, to hope, and to love in its spiritual journey towards the fulfillment of God's promises in the kingdom. New Testament writers depict the community's response to the call of God in Jesus Christ and his Spirit as a lifelong spiritual journey.

# Symbols in the Passion Narrative of
# Mark, Matthew, Luke, and John

| Symbols in the Passion Narratives | OT Background | NT Meaning |
|---|---|---|
| *Mark 14:24* "'this is my blood'" | Blood is a life-principle. The Jewish people were forbidden to consume the blood of animals because God alone is the life-principle for them. | **Jesus** identifies himself with God as **the divine life-principle** for all who accept him. |
| *Mark 14:24* "'the blood of the covenant'" | *Exod 24:3-8* In Israel's official worship the covenant was sealed by a blood rite: half of the blood of the sacrificial animal was sprinkled on the altar, which represented God and half over the people while the Book of the Covenant was read and Moses explained the rite, "This is the blood of the covenant which Yahweh has made with you. . . ." | **Jesus communicates through his death, his covenant-creating and covenant-sustaining life** to integrate all humankind with one another in God (Heb 9:15-21).<br><br>We participate in Jesus' **eschatological banquet community** when we accept his life under the sovereignty of God's love and wisdom as our own. |
| *Mark 14:24* "'. . . poured out for many.'" | 1) *Exod 12:7, 22-23* During the tenth plague, the blood of the lamb put on the lintel and on both door-posts prevented the death of the first born and liberated the Israelites from the bondage of slavery for freedom in the promised land. | Jesus communicates his life which **delivers** humankind **from** bondage *for* communion with God and one another under the sovereignty of God's love. |
|  | 2) *Exod 29:20-21; Lev 8:23, 30* In the rites of consecration for the priest and the altar, the sacrificial blood marked them out as belonging to God. | The life which Jesus communicates **divinizes** humankind through the gift of his Holy Spirit. The godless are made godly. |
| *Matt 26:28* "'This is my blood . . . for the forgiveness of sin'" (cf. *Matt 20:28*). | *Zech 9:11* ". . . because of the blood of your covenant I am sending back your prisoners from the pit (in which there is no water)."<br><br>*Isa 53:12* ". . . surrendering himself to death . . . while he was bearing the faults of many and praying all the time for sinners" | *Emphasizes that Jesus' death overcomes sin, the obstacle to the reception of his life (1 Cor 15:3; Eph 1:7; Col 1:14; Heb 9:22).* |
| *Mark 15:25* "It was the third hour when they crucified him." | Lambs were sacrificed twice daily in the Temple at the time of Jesus, at the third hour (9:00 A.M.) and the ninth hour (3:00 P.M.). | **Jesus is the Lamb sacrificed for all.** (Crucified when the first lambs were sacrificed in the morning and died when the last lambs were sacrificed in the afternoon.) |

| | | |
|---|---|---|
| *Mark 15:34, 37* "Jesus died at the ninth hour." | At this hour trumpets would sound from the Temple calling the faithful to worship God in his holy sanctuary for the sacrifice of the last lamb. | The sacrifice of Jesus, the Lamb of God, is at the heart of Christian worship. |
| *Mark 15:33* "when the sixth hour came there was **darkness** over the whole land until the ninth hour." | *Exod 10:21-31* The liberation of the Hebrews was nearer when God struck the ninth plague over the Egyptians with **three days of thick darkness.** | The **darkness** before Jesus' death lasts **for three hours,** recalling the three days of the primordial liberation event. |
| | Figuratively, darkness represents the state of **alienation and separation from God.** | God achieves his final victory over all that darkness represents through the suffering and dying and rising of Jesus. |
| | Darkness has also an **eschatological sense. The Last Day,** according to Israel's prophets, is one of darkness (Amos 9:9; Jer 15:9; Joel 2:2, 10, 16; 3:4, 16; 4:15; Zeph 1:15). | The darkness and death of Jesus, foreshadowed in the ninth and tenth plagues, represent divine judgment which triumphs over evil and achieves salvation for all mankind. |
| *Mark 15:34; Matt 27:46* "at the ninth hour Jesus cried out in a loud voice . . ., 'My God, my God, why have you forsaken me?'" | The Jewish Temple liturgy took place in the light of day and never in the darkness. The antiphon of the psalms is read by the leader as an invitation to the people to praise God. | Jesus is the new Temple and its new prayer leader. His cry and prayer after the darkness is over implies that God, and not the power of darkness, has the final word about the human condition. |
| | | God achieves his final victory over all the darkness through the suffering, dying and rising of Jesus. That is why in our Mass the phrase "through Christ our Lord" ends all the prayers. The new people of God is in communion with Jesus the new Temple. In Mass, we participate in the self gift of Jesus. |
| *Luke 23:39-43* "The good thief confessed the innocence of Jesus and asked for mercy saying, 'Jesus, remember me when you come into your kingdom.' And Jesus answered, 'In truth I tell you, today you will be with me in paradise.'" | *God remembering his people means God saves, loves and liberates his people.* | *At every Mass we begin with the confession of sin. All Christians are represented by the Good Thief. They are justified in Jesus, the Just One who is dying. And Jesus communicates with us his communion with God. We participate in his invincible life and enjoy his eschatological promise. The tension of the "already and not yet" is felt.* |
| *Luke 23:45-46 (at the ninth hour)* "The veil of the temple was torn right down the middle; and* | *Ps 31 The pious Jews used Psalm 31 as evening or night prayer. Before going to sleep they prayed, "Into your hands I commit my spirit" (v. 5).* | *In Luke there is no mention of destruction of the Temple at the religious trial or in the mocking scene. The rending of the veil is* |

| | | |
|---|---|---|
| when Jesus had cried out in a loud voice saying, 'Father, into your hands I commit my spirit.' With these words he breathed his last." | The Passover ends when the last participant goes to sleep. | placed between Jesus' promise of paradise to the Good Thief and the moment of Jesus' death. Luke shows that Jesus' death is an exodus from the power of darkness and an ascension into glory.<br><br>The rending of the Temple veil before Jesus' death and his quoting Psalm 31:5 emphasizes that Jesus dies in the presence of his Father whom he has made immediately and directly accessible to all through his exodus and ascension.<br><br>Jesus' "exodus" is completed in his death. Unlike Moses, Jesus enters into the promised land; he is assumed by his Father into glory.<br><br>The death of Jesus brings to completion the meaning of the historical Jewish Passover. |
| John 19:23-24 "The soldiers divided Jesus' clothing and threw dice for his seamless garment, thus fulfilling the scripture, 'they shared out my clothing among them. They cast lots for my clothes.'" | Ps 22:18 "they divided my garment among them and cast lots for my clothes."<br><br>According to Jewish traditions, the robes of the high priest and that of Moses and Adam are seamless. And it was forbidden to tear the high priest's garment (Lev 21:10).<br><br>Gen 37:3 Joseph, who was betrayed by his own brother but ultimately became their "saviour," had a coat of long sleeves. | Jesus is priest.<br><br>The Fathers of the Church saw in the seamless garment a symbol of the unity of the Church. |
| John 19:26-27 "Seeing his mother and the disciple he loved standing near her, Jesus said to his mother, 'Woman, this is your son.' Then to the disciple he said, 'This is your mother'. . . ." | | Jesus brings the new family together: the unity of the Church (symbolized by the seamless garment) proceeds from the self-oblation of the Son and the communication of his Spirit in filial love for his heavenly Father and human mother.<br><br>The ultimate meaning and fulfillment of Mary's maternity is revealed in the birth of the new family of God. |

|  |  | The Father and the Son are seen in the giving and receiving of their Spirit (life and love) that unites John and Mary to one another in the dynamic of their trinitarian love. |
|---|---|---|
|  |  | Jesus enables a new way of being and doing and seeing with others. |
| *John 19:28, 34 ". . . Jesus said: 'I am thirsty' . . . one of the soldiers pierced his side with a lance; and immediately came out blood and water."* | *Ps 42:1 "As a doe logs for running streams, so longs my soul for you my God."*<br><br>*Ps 63:1 "God, you are my God, I am seeking you, my soul is thirsting for you, my flesh is longing for you, a land parched, weary and waterless."* | *Water symbolizes the God for whom Jesus thirsts, with whom Jesus is one, and whom he communicates to all through his life-giving death.*<br><br>*The water from his pierced side represents the divine life that he possesses and communicates. It also recalls the eschatological river of life that would satisfy the thirst for God of all humankind.*<br><br>*The effusion of blood and water has a sacramental significance (cf. 1 John 5:6-7). Jesus' mission, guided by the Holy Spirit, began in water beside the Jordan and was consummated in blood upon Golgotha. Christian life, guided by the Holy Spirit, begins in the water of baptism and continues through the blood of the Eucharist; it is a continuing witness to that Love which alone can quench the thirst of all humankind.* |
| *Mark 15:37 "But Jesus gave a loud cry and breathed his last."* | After the darkness had passed, there was the tenth plague, the death of the firstborn male of the Egyptians (Exod 11:5).<br><br>God's judgment in the tenth plague was a vengeance for the Egyptian slaughter of the Hebrews' male children from which Moses was spared (Exod 1:16). It is also a deliverance of the Hebrews from Egyptian bondage.<br><br>The root meaning of "spirit" is "breath," and by extension the life principle of all the living. | Jesus cried out in a loud voice after the darkness had passed. Through Jesus' death God has terminated the state of separation or alienation between Godself and humankind which darkness symbolizes.<br><br>The death of the firstborn and beloved Son of God is the divine judgment for the liberation of all humankind. This time a Jew dies for the Gentiles.<br><br>Jesus' "breathing his last" implies also that he has completed his God-given mission with his communication of the Spirit of God that inaugurated it (cf. Mark 1:11; Ps 2:7; Isa 42:1). |

| | | |
|---|---|---|
| *Mark 15:38* "And the veil of the Sanctuary was torn in two from top to bottom." | God is the most holy and the most separate. Therefore the holiness of God's dwelling place, of the Holy Land and the Holy City required separateness.<br><br>The Temple was divided into many sections on the basis of the degree of separateness between God and humankind. There are courts for the Gentiles, for women, for the Israelites, and for the priests which is the Temple proper. In the center of the Temple, the holy of holiest is the altar and throne of God upon the cherubim. This was entered only once a year, at Yom Kippur, by the high priest (1 Kgs 8:10). God's "face" or presence was veiled within the holy of holiest (Exod 33:11, 14). | God has performed a final act of **saving judgment.** God has destroyed all the barriers between himself and humankind; he has created **a direct access** to himself for all humankind **in Jesus,** his Son, the Beloved (Mark 1:11; 9:7). Alienation has been overcome; communion has been established. **Jesus is the temple,** the heart of divine holiness (Heb 10:19-20).<br><br>**Jesus is the high priest** in the order of Melchizedek (Heb 7:16-17, 24-25). His priesthood stems from his death and resurrection. |
| *Matt 27:51-53 (when Jesus died)* "the veil of the temple was torn in two . . . the **earth quaked** . . . the **tombs opened** and the bodies of many holy people rose from the dead, and these after his resurrection, came out of the tombs, entered the holy city and appeared to a number of people." | *Joel 4:16* "Yahweh roars from Zion, he thunders from Jerusalem; heaven and **earth tremble**."<br><br>*Ezek 37:12-14 the **revival of the dry bones***<br><br>*Dan 12:2 "of those who lie asleep in the dust of the earth many will awake, some to everlasting life, some to shame and everlasting disgrace."* | *The resurrection begins at the death of Jesus. The holy ones of Israel are the first to benefit from Jesus' yielding up (communicating) his spirit for the forgiveness of sin. The final resurrection of all the just has begun. Israel's hope, expressed in Ezekiel's prophecy, is being fulfilled. God is giving his spirit to his people for a rebirth that will enable them to "know God" in the full biblical sense.* |
| *Mark 15:39* "The centurion, who was standing in front of him, had seen how he had died, and he said, 'in truth this man was Son of God.'" | | Through his death, which culminates his mission of suffering and service, Jesus' true identity is manifested. God is no more hidden but **reveals God-self in the Son** (cf. 6:50; 14:62). God's showing God's "face" in God's dying Son is recognized by the Roman centurion who confesses Jesus to be the Son of God. (In Mark, the centurion was the only human who called Jesus "Son of God.")<br><br>The centurion's confession that Jesus is "the Son of God" parallels the voice of God at the baptism and the Transfiguration. |

| | | |
|---|---|---|
| | | The centurion symbolizes: <br>—the efficacy and universal scope of the Servant who gives his life for **all**. <br>—all who make the full Christian confession of faith in Jesus through the power of the Holy Spirit. |
| *Matt 27:54 "The centurion, together with the others guarding Jesus, had seen the earthquake and all that was taking place, and they were terrified and said, 'In truth this man is the Son of God.'"* | | *The confession follows the resurrection of the old covenant saints.* <br><br>*Matthew shows the efficacy of Jesus' death for both Jews and Christians. (In Matthew, Jesus is called 'Son of God' by many. Cf. 14:33; 16:16; 26:63; 27:40, 43.)* |

The evangelists' portrait of Jesus' dying is primarily theology with a transforming purpose so that we may accept Jesus Christ and "participate in the efficacy of his death for all, for the forgiveness of sins, in his exodus from the power of darkness and in his being lifted up for the life of the world."[1] For this purpose, they put together stories, confessions, and proclamations which are rich in symbolic meaning. And in order that they may bear fruit for our transformation, these symbols must first be understood before they can be accepted and assimilated into our lives.[2]

[1] Navone, *Gospel Love,* 44.
[2] The above table on the symbols of the passion narratives is a summary of Fr. Navone's lectures, notes, and books (listed in the bibliography, no. 4) on the topic.

# 9

# Sight to the Blind[1]

Physical sight is a metaphor for spiritual insight in the New Testament. The evangelists presume the historicity of healing the physically blind as part of Jesus' public ministry. They present the accounts of healing from blindness as symbolizing realities that go beyond the physical fact. Their accounts of Jesus giving sight to the blind are a scriptural matrix for a theology of beauty. They ground our understanding of the beauty of God's true goodness as incarnate and revealed in Jesus.

Luke begins and concludes his two-volume work with Old Testament quotations and allusions which implicitly equate response to the mystery of Jesus with seeing the salvation of God (Luke 2:29-32; 3:6; and Acts 28:26-28). When Luke presents Jesus either as enabler or as object of physical seeing, he does so in a way that symbolizes what faith perceives in Jesus and how it acts accordingly. In terms of the theology of beauty, Jesus enables the Christian faith experience of "seeing" the beauty of God's saving and transforming love in human history.

## Jesus as Enabler of Vision

1. Jesus' giving sight to the blind implements the core of the Isaian program orchestrated in Luke 4:18; 7:22; 18:18–19:10.

---

[1] For an extensive treatment of vision as metaphor in Luke, see Dennis Hamm, S.J., "Sight to the Blind: Vision as Metaphor in Luke," *Biblica* 67 (4) (1986) 457–77.

The quotation of Isaiah 61:1-2, applied to the mission of Jesus at Luke 4:18, specifies the proclamation of sight to the blind as the center of the Isaian scenario:

> He stood up to read, and they handed him the scroll of the prophet Isaiah. Unrolling the scroll he found the place where it is written: The spirit of the Lord has been given to me, for he has anointed me. He has sent me to bring the good news to the poor, to proclaim liberty to captives and to the blind new sight, to set the downtrodden free, to proclaim the Lord's year of favor.

Luke 7:18-29 offers a partial commentary on this passage. When the disciples of John the Baptist inquire about Jesus' identity, Jesus points to his healing ministry and describes it by way of allusions to the Isaian visions of the end-time:

> Go back and tell John what you have seen and heard: the blind see again, the lame walk, lepers are cleansed, and the deaf hear, the dead are raised to life, the Good News is proclaimed to the poor and happy is the man who does not lose faith in me (7:22-23).

The healing references are drawn from Isaiah 61:1 (blind, poor); 35:6 (blind, deaf, lame); and 29:18 (blind, deaf, poor). Jesus' answer, therefore, implies that he is the end-time agent who is effecting the end-time healings. Truly to "see" Jesus' healing works is to recognize the work of the eschatological agent/messiah.

2. More Isaian imagery in the prelude: light for the Gentiles, salvation visible (Luke 2:29-32; 3:6).

At the presentation in the Temple, Simeon takes the infant Jesus in his arms and prays the *Nunc Dimittis* (2:29-32), a celebration of Jesus entirely in terms of vision. The words "salvation" *(sōtērion),* "light" *(phōs),* and "glory" *(doxa)* refer to Jesus; for Simeon had been assured by the Holy Spirit (v. 26) that he would not see death until he had seen the Anointed of the Lord. In having Simeon celebrate Jesus in these terms, Luke has him see in the child an identity which will not become evident until the unfolding of volume two of the story (Acts). For Jesus will not fulfill the Isaian hope of being a light to the Gentiles (Isa 42:6–49:6) until he is risen and preaching through his Church (see Acts 13:47 and 26:18, 23).

> Now, Master, you can let your servant go in peace, just as you promised; because my eyes have seen the salvation which you have prepared for all the nations to see, a light to enlighten the pagans and the glory of your people Israel (2:29-32).

Luke's introduction to the Baptist's preaching resumes the motif of seeing the salvation of God (3:6), in the extended quotation of Isaiah 40:3-5: "and all humankind shall see the salvation of God."

3. Three blind men: the rich ruler, the Jericho beggar, and Zaccheus (18:18–19:10).

Significantly, in both the case of the rich ruler (18:24) and Zaccheus (19:5), Jesus both looks at and speaks to both. Luke implies that the true and merciful vision of Jesus can enable the true and loving vision of both. The vision and word of Jesus express his saving grace and call for the transformation of both. The rich ruler, blinded by his attachment to wealth (self-sufficiency), never moves beyond seeing Jesus as "good teacher," an epithet that he applies to Jesus with a meaning that Jesus rejects. The rich ruler's rejection of Jesus' invitation leaves him filled with sadness (18:23); Zaccheus' welcoming of Jesus, in contrast, fills him with joy (19:6). Spiritual blindness entails sadness; spiritual vision/ sight entails joy. Blindness to the beauty of God's true goodness in Christ entails the absence of that joy which true vision alone can give.

Without seeing physically, the blind beggar of Jericho recognizes in Jesus the Son of David, the savior, and the presence of God. This is the faith that opens his eyes and frees his feet to follow: the faith of the supplicant meets the love/mercy of God in Jesus. This illustrates the final verse of the *Benedictus*—"to give light to those who sit in darkness and in the shadow of death, to guide our feet into the way of peace" (1:79). The true disciple "sees" who Jesus truly is and is thereby enabled to follow, praising God. The beggar's anonymity allows the story to become that of every Christian. Called by Jesus personally, he is enabled to see/know him as Lord. With that, Jesus gives the full vision that allows him to follow—praising God and prompting others to follow. There is a paradox in the story of the blind beggar near Jericho (18:35-43): the crowd receives revelation from the blind man who has identified Jesus as "Lord" (v. 41). The hostile "crowd" changes into the people who praise God.

The conversion of Zaccheus (19:1-10) emphasizes the strong desire "to see what kind of man Jesus was" (v. 3). Zaccheus was "too short and could not see" (v. 3) Jesus; so he makes every effort "to catch a glimpse of Jesus" (v. 4) who was to pass that way. The restlessness of Zaccheus to see Jesus implies that, unlike the rich ruler, his wealth has not satisfied him. He seeks a peace and joy beyond himself and his possessions. Resolute in his quest (v. 8), he is finally transformed through faith in Jesus whom he acknowledges as Lord (v. 8). Jesus' seeing and speaking to Zaccheus (v. 5) brings him the joy and peace that he desired.

Both the rich ruler and Zaccheus need to be cured of the kind of blindness associated with their wealth/self-sufficiency. The former clings to his wealth, and becomes sad; the latter adheres to Jesus with joy and resolves to give half his goods to the poor. The encounter with Jesus does not free the rich ruler; it frees Zaccheus, who is open to the light/beauty of God in Jesus.

## Jesus, the Object of True Vision

1. The response to the healing of the paralytic is an instance of true vision: "They were all astounded and praised God, and were filled with awe, saying, 'We have seen strange things today'" (5:26). Within the context of Luke's Gospel, the word "today" is associated with the other "today" sayings which proclaim the presence of salvation (2:11; 4:21; 13:32-33; 19:5, 9; 23:43). What is seen is not merely a marvel but a sign of a divine intervention or "judgment" in human history that, negatively, liberates God's people from evil and, positively, confers to them a good. God visits God's people to deliver them from darkness (alienation) to light (communion with God and all others in God).

2. The apostolic "seeing" or privilege of the disciples is another instance of true vision (10:23-24): "Then turning to his disciples

he spoke to them in private, 'Happy the eyes that see what you see, for I tell you that many prophets and kings wanted to see what you see, and never saw it; to hear what you hear, and never heard it.'" The "seeing" with which the disciples have been blessed is more than the seeing of the external phenomenona of exorcisms (10:17), and the providential protection against evils (10:19). More important, they have been shown, in that experience of the mission, their relationship to the Father and the Son (10:20-22). Their experience of the mission in Jesus' name has been a true vision of Jesus himself.

3. What the healed Samaritan sees is another case of true vision (17:15). Jesus heals ten lepers (17:11-19). It is only to the Samaritan leper that Jesus says, "Your faith has saved (healed) you" (v. 19). The Samaritan leper, "seeing that he was healed came back, praising God with a loud voice, threw himself at the feet of Jesus and thanked him" (17:15-16). Jesus is addressed in the biblical mode for addressing God, heals with a command, and accepts the thanks. The story symbolically affirms that Jesus (not the Temple) has become, for the believer, the proper place for thanking and worshiping God. The healed Samaritan has the true vision of the reign of God that is present in the action and person of Jesus.

4. The lament over and the entry into Jerusalem (13:34-35 and 19:37-38) entail the question of true vision. Jesus' words, "you will not see me until the time comes when you say, 'Blessed is he . . .'" (13:35), will be fulfilled on the occasion of his entry, when it is said that "the whole multitude of the disciples began to rejoice and praise God with a loud voice for all the mighty works they had seen" (19:37-38), saying "Blessed is the King who comes in the name of the Lord!'" Their response to Jesus' healing works is spoken in a "loud voice" like that of the Samaritan leper; it points to a "seeing" that recognizes the works of the Lord, works done by God, in Jesus, hailed as the "king who comes in the name of the Lord." To "see" Jesus, in the context of the lament over unperceiving Jerusalem (13:35), means to perceive him as do the disciples who see him as a nonpolitical king whose reign is evidenced in his healing and who comes in the name of the Lord (19:37-38).

## Fulfillment of Vision at Calvary and Emmaus

1. Calvary: seeing the crucified healer. Luke orchestrates the ways of viewing and the modes of responding among those gathered under the cross. Alluding to Psalm 22:8, Luke speaks of the people standing there looking, while the leaders mock. He writes of the people who have come to see and observe (23:24). And after the death of Jesus and the response of the centurion (who in Luke echoes the response of witnesses to the healing ministry of Jesus by "glorifying God"), "all the crowds who had gathered there for the sight ("spectacle"/*theōrian*), seeing what had happened, returned beating their breasts" (23:48).

Luke would have his reader see this response as paradigmatic of conversion. Their response to the sight they have assembled to see (returning penitentially beating their breasts) recalls the same action of the repentant tax collector (18:13) who went home justified. Their response to the spectacle of the crucified healer is more than what meets the physical eye.

2. The final eye-opening occurs at Emmaus when the risen Lord, "Jesus himself," joins the two on the road to Emmaus. It is said that "their eyes were kept from recognizing him" (24:16). They treat Jesus as an ordinary stranger. They lack that inner kind of vision/seeing called recognition. After Jesus takes, blesses, and shares the bread with them, it is said that their eyes are opened, they recognize him, and he becomes (physically) invisible to them. This restraining of the eyes (24:16) and the opening of the eyes (24:31) is clearly a metaphor for understanding. Jesus had explained to them on the road what was said of him in the Scriptures, how the Christ must die and thus enter into his glory (24:25-27). After the recognition moment, the two say, "Were not our hearts burning when he spoke to us on the road as he opened the Scriptures to us?" (24:32). Recognition or true vision is linked with understanding the Scriptures. This is confirmed later in the appearance to the eleven, when Jesus is said to open their minds (24:45) to understand the Scriptures. It is one step for the disciples to see that the risen one is the Jesus who was crucified. But it is a further step—a deeper vision or seeing—for them to recognize him as the Christ of Scripture who

must suffer and thus enter into his glory. This, for Luke, is truly to see Jesus as he is. Only then do the disciples experience the gift of Easter, and the "eye-witnesses" become ministers of the word (Luke 1:2). Luke's Easter story is the story of that "becoming."

It was not sufficient to see Jesus as a "prophet powerful in word and deed before God and all the people" (24:19). He would finally be seen more fully in the context of the breaking of the bread and the opening of the Scriptures—an understanding which embraces the Messiah's death, his resurrection, and the Church's mission to preach repentance for the remission of sins (conversion) to all the nations (24:46-47). In Acts (26:18), Luke's second volume, that mission will be described as a matter of opening eyes and turning them from darkness to light.

\*　\*　\*

The beauty or glory proper to the God who graciously communicates God's own self to humankind as its truest fulfillment may be seen fully only in God's personal appearance in the form of Jesus Christ. In his cross, no form of beauty by secular standards, God reveals what God's beauty or glory is really about. For eyes which see the cross in the light of the resurrection, God's beauty appears as the glorious love which has extended its reign to include and transform what had been a kingdom of darkness and sin. Luke's canticles proclaim in Jesus right from infancy the rising sun which will illumine those in darkness, the light which will enlighten all humankind, the beauty of that love which is our salvation.

# 10

# Predestined for Glory

The basic themes of the Johannine Scriptures offer a matrix for our understanding of Christian joy in the experience of God's beauty. The Johannine themes imply the relational character of this experience. Through faith we are able to recognize the glory of God in Jesus (2:11; 11:4, 40). Belief in Jesus is belief in the Father who sent him; seeing Jesus is seeing the Father who sent him (12:44-45); welcoming Jesus is welcoming the Father who sent him (13:20). Believing, seeing, and welcoming Jesus are virtually synonymous for expressing the joyful Christian experience of God's beauty/glory in Jesus.

The eternal life hidden in the heart of God from the beginning has become audibly, visibly, tangibly present to us in Jesus; it is the fullness of our joy (1 John 1:1-4). The joy of the Christian community witnesses this reality to the world, that it might share this life. Jesus Christ is the glory and joy of Christian life. The perfect joy which Jesus has, because he is in full communion with the Father (14:20) and does the Father's will (4:34), is to be shared with his disciples (15:11). This he asks from his Father (17:13), and therefore he exhorts his own to abide in him (15:4) and in his love (15:9). His work of self-giving love/life is completed as he lays down his life for his "friends" (15:13). It will only be fully revealed, however, when he goes away from them (16:10). He will not leave them behind as orphans (14:18). He prays the Father to send the Advocate (14:16, 26), manifests himself to them as the risen one (14:19; 20:20 "the disciples rejoiced"), and promises them that prayer in his name will be heard (15:7, 16).

The world cannot take away this joy and consolation any more than it can take away the peace which he gives (14:27; 16:23), for they are grounded in a transcendent reality which does not belong to this world. Christian joy has its source beyond mere earthly, human joy; it is joy in the Spirit of the risen Lord (14:16; 16:14; 19:30; 20:22). Through the risen Lord's gift of his Spirit, our sadness is turned into joy (16:22).

The word which in John's writings most closely approximates our abstract noun "divinity" is that of "glory." Although less precise, the word possesses a greater range of highly concrete overtones owing to its origin in the Old Testament where the "glory of God" described the radiant beauty and overpowering intensity of God's presence and goodness. God was revealing Godself in all the splendor and power that is God's.

John ascribes glory to Jesus "dwelling among us" as an habitual characteristic, for John had "seen" his glory and gives testimony to it (1:14). Glory was evident in Jesus' miracles, which were like signs manifesting it and revealing the supreme power bestowed on him by the Father to indicate that God was present and acting in him (2:11). But, for John, the glory of his supreme goodness shone out most clearly at the passion, the "hour" of the "exaltation" and "glorification" of the Son of Man (12:33-34). This exaltation was itself the sign of the invisible glorification achieved in Jesus by his resurrection, and by which he was finally re-endowed with the glory that he had possessed from the Father before the creation of the world (17:5). Yet this was not the end of the matter, for Jesus wanted his friends to share his glory, and from that moment he communicated to them "the glory you have given me, I have given to them that they may be one even as we are one" (17:22). The principle of unity among the disciples was the glory of Christ radiant among them. Jesus was "glorified in them." Jesus manifests the transfiguring power of his supreme goodness and self-giving love among them. Eventually they would behold Jesus' glory in all its splendor: "Father, I desire that they also, whom you have given me, may be with me where I am, to behold my glory which you have given to me in your love for me before the foundation of the world" (17:24).

John expresses the mystery of Jesus with formulas like Messenger, Son of Man, Son of God, and Word. The word "glory" is a synthesis of all these expressions. It expresses Jesus' very nature, the hidden aspect of being which is revealed to faith alone. Remarkably, John applies to a man a word which formerly described the manifestation in power of Godself. No name like this had ever been bestowed upon prophet, king, priest, or man in the Bible. Never before had a sentence even remotely resembling the following been written about a man: "He manifested his glory, and his disciples believed in him" (2:11). For the glory in the Bible belonged to descriptions of the appearances of God. Only one thing could be meant by applying it to Jesus: God had appeared on earth and had been revealed in all God's power in Jesus. John underscores the essential sameness of the glory of God and the glory of Jesus, for example, "in him (the Son of Man) God is glorified"; "if you believe you will see the glory of God" (13:31; 11:40). These two "glories" are one. John remarks in the prologue to his gospel that it is the interrelation of Father and Son—Jesus' glory was "glory as of the only Son from the Father, full of grace and truth" (1:14). By his use of the word "glory," John understands his gospel as the narrative of a divine appearance, where fire, thunder, and lightning have given place to the appearance of a son of man, Jesus, who called God his Father.

The glory of God manifests the nature, character, and power of God in time, through the incarnate Word. It is the transforming beauty of God's supreme goodness and self-giving love that is enjoyed/seen only by those who have faith. It is a faith-perception of God under the conditions of life in time and space, and the pledge of the ultimate vision of God beyond our historical conditions. Jesus brings the radiance of God within human experience and expresses it most perfectly in his loving self-gift on the cross for our salvation. The glory of the crucified and risen Christ consists in the beauty of the Son's self-surrender to the Father and the Father's love for all humankind. Jesus' prayer that his disciples may behold his glory (17:24) is answered whenever we enjoy the beauty of his self-giving love. The manifestation of God's loving presence and saving power is the vision Jesus has promised to faith (11:40).

John associates the glory of Jesus with the messianic hour or day of salvation. Jesus announces the hour of final triumph for the Son of Man (5:25, 28). It is the hour of perfect worship in the intimate relation with the Father through the Spirit (4:23). Jesus calls it "my hour" (2:4). When "the hour to pass from this world to the Father" (13:1) has come, the hour of a love carried to its term, Jesus goes willingly to his death. He welcomes his hour so that the world may know he loves the Father (14:31). He prays, "Father, the hour has come: glorify your Son so that your son may glorify you" (17:1). This is the hour of both Jesus' death and exaltation. He is raised up on the cross as on a throne of glory. From there he pours his Spirit upon the world in the supreme manifestation and gift of love.

This is the hour when, through the gift of the Spirit, the eye of faith sees the glory of God. When the crucified Son bows his head and gives up his Spirit (19:30), we "see" the Father no less than the Son (14:9) giving us their Holy Spirit of life and love and joy. We see the overwhelming beauty of God's love as the invincible life that is the light of the world, the light shining in the darkness that can never overcome it (1:4-5).

Just as the pillar of fire went on before the Hebrews as they crossed the desert, Jesus is the light which guides the life-journey of the Christian community. The author of the book of Wisdom saw in the pillar of fire a symbol of the "inextinguishable light" of the Law spread across the world by the People of God. Jesus made this observation his own when he announced that he was "the light of the world" (8:12). The original image suggested salvation through the Messiah and everlasting life, but Jesus added, "he who follows me will not walk in darkness, but will have the light of life." The light going on ahead as a guide recalls the pillar of fire, and Jesus is the guide who brings his people to the life he shares with his Father.

In the Johannine Writings the dualism between light and darkness is the context in which Jesus refers to himself as "the light of the world" (John 8:12; 9:5). Persons who follow him in faith do not walk in darkness (estranged from God) but will have "the light of life" (8:12). They will not stumble and fall (11:9-10) but will become "children of the light" (12:36). Being identical with the life of Godself, the preexistent Word was "the light of humankind" whom the darkness could not overcome (1:4-5) neither in the preexistent stage nor when the incarnate Word came into this darkened world for the salvation of humankind (12:46). The guilt of humankind consisted in loving the darkness more than the light (3:19) on account of their evil deeds which made them shun the light (3:20).

Through his self-giving life and death on the cross (1 John 5:6), Jesus offers all humankind the possibility of possessing the light and life of God and demands at the same time that they "walk in the light." This entails our love of one another (1 John 2:9-11). Without this love the affirmation that one is "in light" or in communion with God is devoid of meaning and a lie. Godself is light in whom there is no darkness (1:5). God is love in whom there is no absence of love. God is truth in whom there is no untruth. God is beauty in whom there is no ugliness.

Beginning with Jesus and by means of Jesus who is the "true light" (1:9), but also by means of Christians who have welcomed his light and life and put it into practice through their love for others, God's kingdom of light spreads outwards and forces the darkness to yield. Wherever the Father's self-giving love in Jesus enlightens and transforms human persons, the darkness of unlove is passing away (1 John 2:8). Through the transforming light of Jesus we become the children of light through a creative act of God that recalls the original creation of light. Paul expressed this parallel: "For it is God who said, 'Let light shine out of darkness,' who has shone in our hearts to give the light of the knowledge of the glory of God in the face of Christ" (2 Cor 4:6; cf. Gen 1:3).

The joy of seeing God's glory in all things is at the heart of Christian contemplation and action. The tension between action and contemplation is characteristic of any life in Christ by the power and presence of his Holy Spirit. The beauty of God's love is known in the depths of our hearts both in attentive awareness of God's presence, and in active service through which we participate in the continuing redemptive mystery of Christ. Christian contemplation is not restricted to quiet moments of recollection; nor is it always a private and isolated activity. Rather, Christian contemplation is a way of seeing all things in the light and joy of

Christ's love. It finds its fullest expression in our communion, communication, and community with one another and God.

John's Gospel (especially chapters 14–17) reminds us that Christian contemplation is a way of being. The disciple who sees Jesus and, through him, the One whom Jesus called "Abba," abides in love. And living in the Spirit of Jesus Christ's love purifies our vision of God. Christian contemplation is the joyful vision of God's love, our experience of God's beauty.

Similarly, Paul's writings affirm that those who have faith in Christ and live in his light are bound together in a series of interlocking relationships with love as their source and end. It is the Spirit of Christ's love which makes the disciples one body in Christ. To be "in Christ" is to live in communion with the body by both faith and love.

Both Johannine and Pauline Writings tell us that Christian vision and love are united. God is seen through love. This love is rooted in commitment to God above all, lived out in discipleship which in turn purifies our knowledge of God apprehended first and finally by abiding, dwelling, living in loving communion with God and others.

The central Christian mystery of persons in loving communion, the Trinity, is known and loved not only in quiet reflection, but also in compassionate service for all in need. It is the same Christian mystery contemplated with the look of love, quiet prayer as well as in those activities which heal the human family and build up the body of Christ. The true contemplative sees that God is so intimately involved with all the particulars of creation that this calls for our sharing that involvement. Contemplation is a way of being in which all one's life is a prayer.

## Cosmic Conflict

There is a cosmic conflict in John's Writings between Jesus and the "prince of this world" (John 12:31; 16:11). In the cosmic dialectic between good and evil, experienced in all human life, John underscores the role of Satan (13:2, 27; 14:30) only to proclaim his final defeat. At the very moment when he believes himself certain of victory, the "prince of this world" is "cast down" (12:31).

The love and obedience of the Son triumph over the forces of evil that would deface/deform the beauty of God's true image and likeness in humankind.

God created humankind good and beautiful, conformed to God's goodness/will and wisdom. Through self-will/sin, humankind lost the beauty and goodness of its conformity to the goodness/will and wisdom of God. Jesus Christ, the perfect image and likeness of God, reflects the beauty of God's goodness/will and wisdom ("who sees me, sees the Father"), and transfigures the defaced/deformed image and likeness of God in humankind.

John's basic themes provide a matrix for understanding how the beauty of God in and through Jesus Christ transfigures or "saves" humankind, liberating it from the ugliness and ultimate futility of self-will for the joy of communion in conformity with Beauty Itself/God. Each theme represents an aspect of the beauty of God in Jesus Christ making us beautiful. Each theme expresses an aspect of the joy of God that the beauty of Christ brings to all who are baptized into his life and mission of making all things beautiful. Each theme implies how we glorify God by enjoying God in the beauty of the Son. Even now, within the eschatological tension of our historical pilgrimage, we experience something of that joy and beauty.

The beauty of God's Word/meaning in Christ vs. meaninglessness
The beauty of God's Truth in Christ vs. unreality/mendacity
The beauty of God's Joy in Christ vs. desolation
The beauty of God's Love in Christ vs. hatred
The beauty of God's Life in Christ vs. death
The beauty of God's Sight in Christ vs. blindness
The beauty of God's Voice in Christ vs. deafness
The beauty of God's Way in Christ vs. wandering/aimlessness
The beauty of God's Glory in Christ vs. self-glorification
The beauty of God's Light in Christ vs. the darkness/alienation
The beauty of God's Knowledge in Christ vs. estrangement

## The Gift and Call of Beauty Itself

The mysterious attractiveness of Jesus' person evokes the question of the first disciples: "Where do you live?" (1:38). The power of Jesus to draw us to himself (12:32) is conditioned by the prior drawing by the Father: "No man can come to me unless he is drawn by the Father who sent me" (6:44). And that prior drawing is a listening and learning: "Everyone who has listened to the Father and learned from him, comes to me" (6:35). We cannot recognize the movement of the divine presence in the Son unless we are prepared for such recognition by the presence of the divine Father in ourselves.

The question of the first disciples does not concern Jesus' house; rather, it concerns where and what his life is. Jesus lives "in the Father": "I am in the Father and the Father is in me" (14:10). (The same Greek verb, *menein*/to live, is used in both texts.)

"Come and see," the response of Jesus, invites the disciples to experience for themselves where Jesus lives: ". . . they went and saw where he lived, and stayed with him the rest of the day" (1:39). Christian discipleship means both sharing Jesus' life in the Father and his mission of calling others to that life. The "come and see" of Jesus is what the Father speaks in God's incarnate Word. Jesus is the "come-and-see," the self-gift and call, the grace and invitation of the Father for all humankind. Jesus communicates the mysterious beauty/attractiveness of the Father drawing all humankind to Godself.

The mysterious beauty of the Father drawing us to Godself in Jesus is shared by the disciples of Jesus. Philip, immediately after his welcoming the gift and call of Jesus, calls Nathanael to "come and see" Jesus (1:46). When Nathanael "sees" and proclaims that Jesus is the "Son of God" and the "king of Israel" (1:49), Jesus announces that he will see even greater things (1:50): "You will see heaven laid open and, above the Son of Man, the angels of God ascending and descending" (1:51). Alluding to both Jacob's ladder (Gen 28:12) and to Daniel's Son of Man (Dan 7:13-14), Jesus indicates that he is the mediator between God and humankind, the new Jacob's ladder through whom God descends to us and we ascend to God. In other words, Jesus is the way to meet/know God.

The same mysterious beauty of the Father in Jesus transforms the Samaritan woman. Welcoming Jesus' revelation to her, "I am he" (4:26)—an allusion to the theophany Moses experienced (Exod 3:14)—the Samaritan tells the people, "Come and see" (4:30). In Jesus is now revealed glory/beauty (John 1:14) whose reflection illuminated the face of Moses after his encounters with God (Exod 34:29-35). Whoever truly believes in Moses also believes in Jesus (John 5:45-47). His countenance, like that of Moses, reflects the glory/beauty of the Lord who transforms us into his own image (2 Cor 3:18). To see the glory of Jesus—"that is his as the only Son of the Father, full of grace and truth" (1:14)—entails both the revelation of the Father ("the only Son of the Father") and our salvation ("full of grace and truth").

Faith is the precondition for contemplating the beauty of the Father's face and for enjoying the beauty of the Father's voice in Jesus:

> ". . . the Father who sent me
> bears witness to me himself.
> You have never heard his voice,
> you have never seen his face,
> and his word finds no home in you
> because you do not believe
> in the one he has sent" (5:37-38).

Mary Magdalene recognizes the risen Lord by the sound of his voice (20:16). She tells the disciples that she has seen the Lord (20:18). The sight of the risen Lord fills the disciples with peace and joy (20:20). Enjoying God's beauty in the risen Lord is the distinguishing characteristic of all Christian life/experience.

For John, Jesus is the glory of God; therefore he speaks of believers as those who have seen Jesus' glory (cf. 1:14; 2:11). To know God/Jesus, for John, is to enjoy the beauty/glory of God/Jesus.

# Part III

## BEAUTY IN THE CHURCH

# 11

## Edwards and Aquinas

### I

Jonathan Edwards (1703–58), American philosopher, theologian and Congregational pastor, was born in East Windsor, Connecticut. He was educated at Yale and succeeded his grandfather as minister of the congregational Church at Northampton, Massachusetts (1727–50). Renowned for his powerful preaching and hardline Calvinism, he helped inspire the revivalist movement known as the "Great Awakening." He was dismissed in 1750 for his overzealous orthodoxy and became a missionary to the Housatonnuck Indians at Stockbridge, Massachusetts, and eventually in 1757 became president of the College of New Jersey (now Princeton University). He is regarded as the greatest theologian of American puritanism, his main doctrinal work being the *Careful and Strict Enquiry into the Modern Prevailing Notions of that Freedom of the Will* (1754).

Throughout his pastoral career, but especially during the Great Awakening, Edwards was especially concerned about the central question of puritanism: how shall the presence of the Divine Spirit be discerned? He not only asserted against the opponents of revivalism that true religion consisted in "holy affections," but he also provided, against those enthusiasts who had reduced religion to a false emotionalism, criteria for testing true religious affections. Although "affections" included emotions, passions, and the will, they were more essentially that which moved a person to accept the divine majesty. Love was the chief affection and the foundation of all others, internal as well as external.

Edwards affirmed that there were no infallible signs that could publicly test the fruits of the Divine Spirit; nevertheless, he discerned some signs that were helpful to the individual as guides in discovering the presence of saving grace. Spirituality was an inward experience that inexorably became outward in practice and therefore was somewhat public and verifiable.

Edwards, in his *Religious Affections* (1746), described twelve signs he discovered in Scripture and reason that could help the individual discern the presence of the Divine Spirit. Some signs pointed to the cause of affections, others to affections themselves, and still others to their consequences. Affections are truly holy if, among other things, they are spiritual, born of the Spirit, who produces a new spiritual sense—a "new foundation laid in the nature of the soul"; manifest a genuine love to God that has no other intention than the transcendently excellent nature of the divine glory; arise from enlightened minds that have a taste for and commitment to the divine beauty; are accompanied with a positive conviction of divine reality and with an evangelical humility; transform human nature by turning it from sin to holiness; beget meekness, quietness, forgiveness, and mercy; produce fear and joy in symmetry and proportions; increase the spiritual appetite creating a longing of the soul after spiritual attainments; and persistently and perseveringly produce fruits of Christian practice in which behavior in the world is conformed to and directed by the Christian vision of reality. Christian practice was not just the realization of faith, but an essential and inherent part of the inner religious experience of the Holy Spirit. Christian action, in fact, was the paramount sign, but not the cause, of true spirituality and activity in the world. The affections themselves were always signs of something more ultimate—God and the Spirit. The regeneration of the world, like the renewal of the Christian life, was the result of the new outpouring of God's Spirit.

In New England, Edwards became the most brilliant spokesman for the "Great Awakening," the religious ferment or revival that emerged in the English colonies in America during the second quarter of the eighteenth century. The Awakening is sometimes dated as occurring between 1739 and 1742. Those who experienced the revival often described it as a conversion and expressed it by emotional manifestations such as weeping, fainting, and physical gyrations. The Awakening preachers worked for a "New Birth." They tended to define religion more in terms of religious experiences than in terms of religious beliefs or doctrines. The Great Awakening was a democratic movement in the sense that it insisted that all Christians should have the Christian religious experience. This experience often took the form of direct visions of God or Satan, unintelligible shrieking and violent body movements among the worshipers.

Edwards' study at Yale had brought him under the influence of John Locke, for whom experience, and not innate ideas, was the starting point for serious thinking. This meant for Edwards that the truth of theological assertions was not to be found in the free speculation of the mind but in the actual experience of that with which the assertions dealt. The goodness of God, for example, cannot be believed simply because someone says God is good; it can only be believed if one experiences the goodness of God.

If Edwards was a busy pastor and preacher, he was also a philosopher critically reflecting upon and sharply questioning much of the activity in the Great Awakening. In a series of sermons preached in 1742 he noted how urgent it was that Christians be able to tell gold from dross in religious experience. These sermons were later published as the *Treatise on Religious Affections* (1746).

Edwards was fascinated by the discoveries of Newton and his successor. Yet, fearing the drift of such ideas into materialism, he argued that the laws of science were not self-subsisting. Rather, they were products of God's self-conscious intellectual activity. Edwards was not threatened by the discoveries of science because he felt they revealed the regularity, harmony, and beauty of the Divine Being.

His theological system was of thoroughgoing trinitarian pattern and content. By a revisionary use of Locke's epistemology, Edwards freed Newtonian physics from mechanistic interpretation. He thereupon found in it no obstacle to trinitarian faith but instead a vision of cosmic eventful harmony exactly appropriate to the triune God, who *is* the harmony of perfect community among Father, Son, and Spirit. God and creation are each beautiful, in the way that a fugue is beautiful. It is God's musical beauty that is God's very deity, and the creation's corresponding beauty that is its value to God and therefore its being.

The unifying center of Edwards' theology was the glory of God depicted as an active, harmonious, ever-unfolding source of absolutely perfect Being marked by supernal beauty and love. The dynamic activity of the Godhead, especially as manifest in the Trinity, was ever in the forefront of his work. He promoted an affectional view of reality in which "the sense of the heart" (one of his favorite phrases) was foundational for thought and action alike. Living faith involved much more than facts about God, it also required a new "taste" of divine beauty, holiness, and truth. Moral behavior, in the strictest sense, arose only from a heart regenerated by God's mercy. He contrasted this behavior with a kind of morality that was merely a prudential, pragmatic expression of self-love.

## II

The psalmist confessed that his glimpses of the Lord made sense of his life: "One thing have I desired of the Lord, that I will seek after . . . to behold the beauty of the Lord" (Ps 27:4). The Christian philosophy of Jonathan Edwards proposed that beauty is God's most distinctive characteristic because it conveys the expressive, self-giving, and endlessly delightful character of God. In his reflections upon the Great Awakening, Edwards became convinced that the experience of beauty is the key to the encounter between God and persons and that it is fundamental to human motivation.

Edwards associated beauty with the sense of taste. When he refers to the "loveliness and sweetness . . . of the Divine nature," he stressed God's availability to human experience.[1] With this

---

[1] "A Divine and Supernatural Light," *Jonathan Edwards: Representative Selections,* eds. Clarence H. Faust and Thomas H. Johnson (New York: Hill and Wang, 1962) 108. "A Treatise of Grace," quoted in Roland André Delattre, *Beauty and Sensibility in the Thought of Jonathan Edwards: An*

same sense the psalmist invites us to "taste and see that the Lord is good" (Ps 34:8). Since taste requires openness, we will not experience the beauty of God if we are closed within ourselves. The experience of beauty also resembles the experience of taste in that it is immediate. Taste is not usually a matter for reflection. Edwards states that what we call beautiful is "immediately pleasant to the mind."[2]

In his treatise *Freedom of the Will,* Edwards argues that the will is operative as we are drawn affectionately toward an object of delight. Beauty stimulates intellectual activity.

> It engages the attention of the mind. . . . The beauty and sweetness of objects draws on the faculties, and draws forth their exercises; so that reason itself is under far greater advantages for its proper and free exercises, and to attain its proper end, free of darkness and delusion.[3]

Beauty, for Edwards, engages the affections, motivates thought and action, and thereby creates relationships. He believed that the goal of human life is affectionate engagement with God—Beauty Itself—above all, and with all existence.

Edwards realized that we all begin with particular beauties, since our perceptions of beauty are personal, bound by our own time, place, and other limiting characteristics. He believed that it was God's grace that helped us to expand our experiences, interrelating particular perceptions into more inclusive perspectives, seeing new beauties of a more comprehensive character: "We are apt, through the narrowness of our views, in judging of the beauty of affections and actions to limit our consideration to only a small part of the created system."[4] For Edwards the most comprehensive vision of beauty reveals the beauty of God: "The nature of true virtue consists in a disposition to benevolence towards being

---

*Essay in Aesthetics and Theological Ethics* (New Haven: Yale University Press, 1968) 28.

[2] Jonathan Edwards, *The Nature of True Virtue* (Ann Arbor: University of Michigan Press, 1960) 98–9.

[3] Edwards, "A Divine and Supernatural Light," 108.

[4] Edwards, *The Nature of True Virtue,* 88.

in general."[5] He believed that beauty was at the heart of the experience that opens persons to God: "God is God, and distinguished from all other beings and exalted above them, chiefly by His divine beauty."[6] He implies that God is actively engaged with all creation through God's beauty. Creation, love, providence, and redemption express the reality of Beauty itself: what Beauty is and does. The psalms affirm that the Lord shines forth, that God is self-giving, engaging, and outgoing: God is not self-absorbed and indifferent (e.g., Ps 27:1).

Beauty shows itself; it shines forth, eager to be seen and known. Edwards identifies the Holy Spirit with the divine beauty:

> It was made especially the Holy Spirit's work to bring the world to its beauty and perfection out of the chaos: for the beauty of the world is a communication of God's beauty. The Holy Spirit is the harmony and excellence and beauty of the deity. Therefore, it was his work to communicate beauty and harmony to the world, and so we read that it was He that moved upon the face of the waters.[7]

God's self-giving is God's perfection, the essence of God's beauty: "The glory of God is the shining forth of His perfections. The world was created that they might shine forth—that is, that they might be communicated."[8] Not only does God manifest God's beauty, but as Edwards affirms, "He delights in communicating His happiness to the creature."[9] God enjoys being God, our self-giving origin-sustainer-destiny. God's beauty is our joy, and our joy proclaims God's beauty.

Jonathan Edwards interpreted God's righteousness as God's moral beauty. He identified God's beauty with God's self-giving

[5] Ibid., 5.

[6] Edwards, "Religious Affections," *Works of Jonathan Edwards,* ed. John E. Smith (New Haven: Yale University Press, 1959) 2:298.

[7] From "Miscellanies," no. 293 in the Yale Collection of Edwards' manuscripts (Yale University Library). Quoted in Delattre, *Beauty and Sensibility,* 152.

[8] Edwards, "Miscellanies," no. 247. Quoted in Delattre, *Beauty and Sensibility,* 177.

[9] Edwards, "Miscellanies," no. 1151. Quoted in Delattre, *Beauty and Sensibility,* 177.

love which Jesus revealed from the heart of God.[10] The beauty of
the Lord engages us; for the heart of the Lord is not self-contained
but expressive, outgoing, and loving. God's righteousness shines
forth, creating and loving and establishing communion among
persons and between them and God. Edwards identified God's
beauty with the truth that God is a communicating God whose
essence is self-communication.[11] When Edwards thought about
how God spoke so joyfully through the angels to announce the
birth of Jesus, he concluded that God's desire to communicate did
not derive from any want or deficiency in Godself that God
should stand in need of another, but from God's infinite fullness
which overflows to all creatures.[12] God's beauty has priority for
Edwards over God's self-sufficiency; for beauty is the heart of
God. It is God's loving radiance, engaging, giving forth, inspiring
and joyful self-giving. The infinite goodness and happiness of
God beautifully irradiate all creation.[13] All creation is an expression of God's beauty. The joyful beauty of the Creator affects
creatures. As God "delights in glorifying Himself," Edwards affirmed, it is "beautiful that infinite brightness and glory should
shine forth"; thus "God delights in communicating His happiness
to the creatures," and in doing so God "enjoys Himself."[14]

The greatest beauty, Edwards concluded, is in the act of beautifying—bringing others to fulfillment. The beauty of God burst
forth into creativity. If sin corrupts relationships, the beauty of
God restores them. The greatest beauty occurs when God reaches
out to rescue and transform the fallen, opens human hearts to believe and to hope and to love, and gives hope of final communion

[10] R. Cartwright Austin, *Beauty of the Lord* (Atlanta: John Knox Press, 1987) 125–6.

[11] Edwards, "Miscellanies," nos. 332 and 107. Quoted in Delattre, *Beauty and Sensibility,* 170.

[12] Edwards, "Sermon on Luke 2:14." Quoted in Delattre, *Beauty and Sensibility,* 170.

[13] Edwards, "A Dissertation Concerning the End for Which God Created the World," *The Works of President Edwards,* S. E. Dwight (New York: S. Converse, 1829) 3:20.

[14] Edwards, "Miscellanies," no. 1151. Quoted in Delattre, *Beauty and Sensibility,* 177.

among all humankind. The crucified Christ reveals God's beauty beautifying all humankind in the work of redemption, the new creation which recalls the joy of God in the first creation (Gen 1:12, 32).

The historian Amanda Porterfield calls attention to the relationship of divine beauty and marriage in the lives of New England Puritans, including Jonathan Edwards:

> One of the most striking phenomena about the New England Puritans is that their greatest ministers and governors—Thomas Shepard, John Winthrop, Simon Bradstreet, Edward Taylor, and Jonathan Edwards, for example—loved their wives beyond measure. These men found their wives to be earthly representatives of God's beauty. For these men a loving wife was not only a model Christian but also an expression of the beauty of the world that pointed beyond itself to divine beauty. And the enjoyment of God's beauty was the essence of Puritan spirituality.[15]

Edwards believed that the experience of God's moral beauty elicits human awakening. He called this the "beauty of holiness": "A love of divine things for the beauty and sweetness of their moral excellency, is the first beginning and spring of all holy affections. . . . The beauty of holiness . . . is the quality that is the immediate object" of human awareness in the experience of the Lord. Edwards states that it is when we sense "the beauty of the moral perfection of Christ" that we can accept Jesus as mediator, reconciling us to God.[16] The real believer is one who falls in love with the beauty of God:

> The first foundation of a true love to God, is that whereby he is in himself lovely, or worthy to be loved, or the supreme loveliness of his nature. . . . How can that be true love of beauty and brightness, which is not for beauty and brightness' sake?[17]

Our participation in God's delight and beauty results from God's manifestation of God's beauty. God's beauty beautifies and

[15] A. Porterfield, *Feminine Spirituality in America: From Sarah Edwards to Martha Graham* (Philadelphia: Temple University Press, 1980) 49.
[16] Edwards, "Religious Affections," 253–4, 260, 273.
[17] Ibid., 242–3.

delights our lives: "God delights in communicating His happiness to the creature."[18]

## III

From his early years as a student Edwards had made beauty his special concern. He wrote in his notebook: "(Beauty) is what we are more concerned with than anything else."[19] As a mature theologian he chose it as the best way to describe the divine nature. Beauty, he concluded, is that in which "the truest idea of divinity does consist." Again, "God is God, and distinguished from all other beings, and exalted above 'em, chiefly by his divine beauty, which is infinitely diverse from all other beauty."[20]

Edwards' theology of beauty is set within the tradition of Thomas Aquinas. Both agree that God is Happiness Itself. Aquinas affirms that in God alone is it true that God's very being is God's being happy.[21] Whatever God is, is God's happiness; this is not something extrinsic to God, but God's very life or eternal activity. The triune God, for both Aquinas and Edwards, eternally delights in the beauty of the divine true goodness. The delightful character of God is for both the eternal delight of the blessed.

Edwards concurs with Aquinas's view that the beautiful is "that which when seen gives delight/pleasure"; and that the "seeing" and "pleasure" of God's delight in God's beauty is not physical, because "God is spirit" (John 4:24).[22] The divine and human "seeing" of and "delight" in beauty are essentially spiritual; both

---

[18] Edwards, "Miscellanies," no. 1151. Quoted in Delattre, *Beauty and Sensibility,* 177.

[19] Jonathan Edwards, "Notes on the Mind," Vol. 1, *The Philosophy of Jonathan Edwards from his Private Notebooks,* ed. Harvey G. Townsend (Eugene: University of Oregon Press, 1955).

[20] Edwards, "Religious Affections," 2:298.

[21] Aquinas, *Summa Theologiae,* I–II, q. 3, a. 2. "Perfect happiness belongs naturally to God alone, as in Him being and happiness are identical. For the creature, however, happiness is not a natural possession but its last end" (*ST* I, q. 62, a. 4).

[22] *ST* II–II, q. 152, a. 4, ad 3. Some observations of Aquinas regarding delight: "It is good in the highest degree because it is perfect rest in a sublime

108 *Enjoying God's Beauty*

entail the cognitive and affective consciousness of knowing and
loving subjects.

Edwards and Aquinas agree that Beauty Itself (God or Supreme
Beauty) is the origin and ground and perfection of all created
beauty; that Beauty Itself is equally Truth and Goodness Itself.
The good and true and being, Aquinas affirms, are one and the
same reality, but in the mind they are distinguished from each
other.[23] "The beauty of the creature," writes Aquinas in his commentary on the *Divine Names* of Dionysius, "is nothing else than
the likeness of the divine beauty participated in things."[24] Creaturely beauty, then, like the divine beauty which is its source, will
lie in the actuality of being or existence.

Edwards' affirmation of the self-giving and expressive character
of the divine beauty squares with Aquinas's teaching that God's
motive in creation was the diffusion of God's goodness: being
good, God wanted to share God's goodness with others. In the
context of the *Divine Names,* Aquinas claims that the divine
beauty is the motive of creation. Because God loves God's own
beauty, God wishes to multiply it as far as possible by communicating God's likeness to creatures. God is the cause of their radiance by sending down to all of them a share of God's luminous
ray. Each form imparted to a creature is a beautifying participation
in the divine radiance, "a kind of irradiation coming forth from the
divine brilliance"; and since being *(esse)* comes from form, we can
say that beauty is the fount of the existence of all things.[25]

---

good" (*ST* q. 34, a. 3, ad 3); it arises from a real union with the good (*Summa
contra Gentiles* 1, 90): it arises from love for someone/something (*ST* I–II,
q. 31, a. 6).

[23] *ST* I–II, q. 29, a. 5.

[24] *In Div. Nom.,* c. 4. lect. 5. nn. 352–4.

[25] "Quomodo autem Deus sit causa claritatis, ostendit (Dionysius) subdens,
quod Deus immittit omnibus creaturis, cum quodam fulgore, traditionem sui
radii luminosi, qui est fons omnis luminis; quae quidem traditiones fulgidae
divini radii, secundum participationem, similitudinis sunt intelligendae et
istae traditiones sunt pulchrificae, id est facientes pulchritudinem in rebus."
Ibid., n. 340. "Dicit (Dionysius) ergo primo quod ex pulchro isto (i.e., Dei)
provenit esse omnibus existentibus . . . unde patet quod ex divina pulchri-
tudine esse omnium derivatur." Ibid., n. 349.

Edwards concurs with Aquinas's teaching that the divine beauty is the cause of the harmony and order in the universe. Beauty wields a power over all things, giving them whatever unity they have: unity of actions, mutual adaptations, containments, and concretions; among rational creatures their agreement/harmony in mind and heart or true friendship.[26]

Edwards' theology of beauty also concurs with Aquinas's teaching that Beauty Itself (God) exercises three kinds of causality. Out of love for God's own beauty God acts as an efficient cause, giving existence to everything, and moving and conserving them. God is also, in God's beauty, the final cause of the universe, for God created it so that it might, to the extent possible, imitate God's own beauty. Finally, Beauty Itself is the exemplar cause of everything, creating each thing and distinguishing it from every other in accord with Its beautiful ideas. God creates the universe to make it beautiful.[27]

Both Edwards and Aquinas affirm that God is Beauty Itself, the source of all created beauty, containing in a superlative way all the marks of the beautiful. God is eternally and invariably beautiful. God is entirely beautiful, unlike creatures, whose beauty is often partial and mingled with ugliness. Each creature has a special nature of its own and hence a particular beauty, whereas God's loveliness, like God's nature, is infinite. Unlike temporal things God is not beautiful at one time and not at another, or in one respect and not in another. Nor is God's beauty conditioned by place. Some things are beautiful in one place and not in another, for they seem beautiful to some people and not to others, but God is beautiful in the sight of everyone and without qualification.[28]

Both Edwards and Aquinas consider beauty to be one of the essential names of God, who beautifies all creation. Aquinas interprets the six days of creation in Genesis as six stages in the

[26] "Propter pulchrum divinum sunt omnium rationalium creaturarum concordiae, quantum ad intellectum concordant enim qui in eamden sententiam conveniunt; et amicitiae, quantum ad affectum; et comuniones, quantum ad actum vel ad quodcumque extrinsecum; et universaliter omnes creaturae, quantamcumque unionem habent, habent ex virtute pulchri." Ibid., n. 349.
[27] Ibid., nn. 352, 354.
[28] Ibid., n. 345.

developing beauty of the cosmos.[29] Creation entails a progressive beautification of the heavens and the earth. Their natural loveliness would not last forever; it was destined to be transfigured and glorified, along with the elect and the world itself, at the end of time. The universe would always continue to exist, but it would be transformed in the glory of heaven. When asked why the universe itself should remain in a gloried state, Aquinas replied that it is fitting because it is mainly through its loveliness (beauty) that we come to know God its creator.[30] This same conviction is at the heart of Edwards' theology of God's redemptive, transfiguring, joy-giving beauty.

[29] See *De Potentia,* IV, 2; *ST* I, q. 66, a. 1c. The succession Aquinas envisages in the six days of creation is on the part of creatures, not on the side of God or God's act of creation. The act itself is not successive since it does not imply movement. See *Contra Gentiles,* II, 19.

[30] *In IV Sent.,* d. 48, q. 2, a. 3; ed. Vivès 11:450. God knows and loves God's creation and enjoys its beauty. God's enjoyment is not a response to created beauty, it is its cause.

# 12

---

# Beauty in Liturgy

Our Christian worship of God implies a relationship between ourselves and God. It is the relationship of the creature, made in the image of God, and the Creator. Outside this relationship, we would cease to be. The proper relationship between creature and Creator is, in Christian eyes, the relationship of worship. Christian worship shows us the Christian view of both humankind and God.

Our being made in the image of God implies that God has made us sufficiently like Godself for communion between God and ourselves to be possible. God's gracious call to communion with Godself includes both the initial and basic capacity, the aided progress in time, and the final and eternal realization.

The ultimate goal of the human vocation is enunciated in clearly liturgical terms in the opening question and answer of the Westminster Shorter Catechism (1647–48):

> What is the chief end of man?
>
> Man's chief end is to glorify God, and to enjoy him for ever (John 17:21-23; Rom 11:36; 1 Cor 10:31; Ps 73:25-28).

*Glory* denotes both God's excellence and God's splendor. It is the sign of God's active presence among us. We may render God glory as we are changed into God's likeness, "from glory to glory" (2 Cor 3:18). We glorify God as we grow in conformity with God's goodness. We ourselves thereby become glorified. The glorious bodies hoped for in the final resurrection bespeak this ultimate realization of the human vocation. God will thereby be glorified because God's intention will have been achieved. Communion with God, the transfiguration/divinization of our life through the gift of the Holy Spirit: this is experienced as the enjoyment of God. Scriptures often express the enjoyment of our glorified life in terms of taste. The believer feeds on the will/love of God, "man does not live by bread alone but by every word that proceeds from the mouth of God" (Deut 8:3). The psalmist confessed that God's words were "sweeter than honey to my mouth" (Ps 119:103). The invitation from another psalm, "O taste and see that the Lord is good" is echoed in two New Testament passages:

> Those who have been enlightened, who have tasted the heavenly gift, and have become partakers of the Holy Spirit, and have tasted the goodness of the word of God and the powers of the age to come . . . (Heb 6:4-5).

> Like newborn babes, long for the pure spiritual milk, that by it you may grow up to salvation; for you have tasted the kindness of the Lord (1 Pet 2:2-3).

We are transformed by feeding on the word of God. Jesus affirms that "My meat is to do my Father's will" (John 4:32-34). The obedience of the Cross was both Jesus' glorification of the Father and his own glorification (John 17:1-5). The unity of Father and Son is a unity of mutual knowledge (John 10:15) and common operation (5:17, 19, 20). It is a unity of willing/loving and knowing. Jesus' loving self-surrender to God reveals the self-giving love of God's nature. On the cross it is finally revealed who God is and what the world is (Rev 13:8; cf. 1 Pet 1:20). In Christian eyes, Jesus Christ is the embodiment of the relationship God intends should obtain between humankind and Godself. He is the recipient, the mediator, and the pattern of Christian worship, revealing the Christian vision of both humankind and God.

The abiding presence and significance of Jesus Christ in history can be described by means of the traditional doctrine of his three offices. Jesus Christ, through his Spirit, is the way (shepherd and king), the truth (prophet and teacher), and the life (priest) of the world (John 14:6).

The Old Testament speaks of God as light (Ps 27:1; 2 Sam 22:29; Isa 60:19). God's law is a lamp to the feet and a light to the path (Ps 119:105). The New Testament takes up this message. Jesus is designated as the eschatological prophet (Deut 18:15) promised in the Old Testament (Acts 3:22; John 1:45; 6:14). Similarly, he is known as a teacher (e.g., John 13:13), as light of the world (John 1:9; 8:12; 12:46), as truth (14:6), as the final revelation of God (Heb 1:1-2). He opposed lies and darkness, which are the consequence of sin (Rom 1:18-20; John 1:5; 3:19; 8:44; 1 John 3:8). Consequently, Christ's Spirit is called the Spirit of truth (John 14:17; 15:26; 16:13), of faith (2 Cor 4:13), of wisdom and of revelation, who enlightens the eyes of our heart, so that we may understand our vocation and inheritance (Eph 1:17-18).

It would be interesting to trace the history of the symbolism of light in the Christian liturgy and its application to Jesus Christ who is celebrated in the Easter Vigil as light, at Christmas and Epiphany as *sol invictus*. The liturgical tradition clarifies what it means to say that Jesus Christ is light, truth, prophet, and teacher. In him the truth about God, humankind, and the world has definitely become manifest, and his Spirit is for all who believe the *Lumen cordium* (Pentecost sequence, *Veni Sancte Spiritus*). Through him the meaning of human existence has been definitively disclosed. Through the light of his truth we can get our bearings in this life and find our way. His light is our salvation. We are enlightened by the abiding presence of Christ's truth in the world through the Spirit, whose function it is to recall Christ's words and works and, by bringing them to remembrance, to keep them present (John 14:26; 16:13-14).

Life is another aspect of the abiding presence and meaning of Jesus Christ in history. Life in this context is always more than purely biological. Life includes our questions about life, about authentic, fulfilled, true life. Life longs for the light of life. Since life is constantly threatened by decay and death, we are concerned about abiding, eternal life.

The Old Testament affirmed that God alone is the source and Lord of life (cf. 1 Sam 2:6; Job 12:9; Deut 32:39; Ps 104:29). God's life appeared in Jesus Christ (John 1:4; 5:26; 11:25; 14:6; 1 John 1:1; 5:11); he is sent to bring life to the world (John 3:15-16;

10:10). One who believes in him already has life (John 5:24; 1 John 3:14). Similarly, one who loves the brethren has passed out of death into life (1 John 3:14; 4:7, 12, 16). The life that has appeared in Jesus Christ is ultimately revealed in Jesus' sacrifice on the cross and in his resurrection from the dead (Rom 6:10; 14:9; 2 Cor 13:4). Death is finally defeated thereby (Rom 5:10) and life opened for those who believe (Rom 1:17; 6:8-10; Gal 3:11; Heb 10:38). This life is bestowed on us in the Spirit. For the Spirit is God's vital creative power by which Christ was raised from the dead. The life of the risen Christ therefore dwells in believers through the Spirit given them in baptism (Rom 8:2, 10; Gal 6:8). The Spirit is the first fruits (Rom 8:23) and the guarantee (2 Cor 1:22; 5:5) of eternal life.

The three offices of Jesus indicate ways in which his Spirit enables us to enjoy God's beauty. God's Spirit attracts and draws us to Jesus as shepherd and king by enabling us to see and to joy in the beauty of his supreme goodness. God's Spirit draws us to Jesus as our prophet and teacher by enabling us to recognize and rejoice in the beauty of his truth. God's Spirit draws us to Jesus as our priest by enabling us to joy in the beauty of communion with him in worshiping God in spirit and truth. God's Spirit enables our joyful contemplation of God's presence and action in human life, history, world, and Church. It enables us to see the beauty of the Spirit in the fruits of the Spirit: love, joy, peace, patience, kindness, goodness, faithfulness, gentleness, and self-control (Gal 5:19-23; cf. Rom 14:17).

It is the mystery of Jesus Christ that the Church proclaims and celebrates in its liturgy so that the faithful may live from it and bear witness to it for the joyful transfiguration of the world. In the celebration of the liturgy, the Church shares in Christ's prophetic (proclamation) and kingly (service of charity) priesthood (worship). Through the liturgy we enjoy the beauty of "the great love with which the Father has loved us" in God's beloved Son (Eph 2:4).

The liturgy is a form of our communion in Christ's own prayer to the Father in the Spirit. Christ is the fundamental Sacrament, the primordial communion of the divine and human. Christian worship takes place "in Christ" as the locus of the saving divine and human communion-community-communication that is our

God-given destiny. Enjoying the beauty of God "in Christ" is, even now, a proleptic experience of Eternal Love, Eternal Life, Happiness Itself.

The liturgy is the matrix of the Christian faith-vision and faith-expectation of reality. The liturgy is where that vision and expectation find concrete expression. The Christian community worships with the conviction that the kingdom of God has come and will "one day" be incontestably and irrevocably established as what is most real/true/good/beautiful. The hope of the Christian community is based on indications that, "in Christ," reality is in fact being transformed in that direction. The liturgy is where the Christian community proclaims and celebrates the reasonable grounds for its ultimate expectations.

The substance of the Christian faith-vision and faith-expectation in the liturgy concerns the relationship the Christian community believes that God intends should obtain between ourselves and Godself. The divine purpose for humankind is fundamental to Christian vision and expectation. The Christian community recognizes Jesus Christ as the embodiment of the true and definitive relationship for our communion with God. Occupying the central place in Christian worship, Jesus Christ is the recipient and mediator and pattern for worship. The Spirit of the Father and Son that has been poured into our hearts (Rom 5:5) enables a worship in conformity with Christ. The Spirit enables the divine work of transformation required if human beings are freely to enter into God's purposes for them. The communal character of humankind in God's purpose is witnessed by the body of Christ and the temple of the Spirit. The worship of the Christian community expresses the eschatological tension which marks its way to the achievement of God's purpose.

The human vocation to communion with God bears an inescapably social character. Christ attracted to himself a body of disciples whom he called communally to follow his way to the Father. The Spirit has continued to inspire and enable people to join in adopting the pattern defined by Christ for the achievement of the divine kingdom and human salvation.

The heart of society, whether human or divine, is love. The image of God in humankind is then the God-given capacity to love.

Divine love for humankind and human love for God have always been seen by the Christian community to imply the love of human beings for one another. Baptism, for example, is the sacrament of entry into a new set of family relationships. Rebirth as sons and daughters of God implies the acquisition of new brothers and sisters in the persons of all the Father's children. This is the basis of that "love of the brethren" *(philadelphia)* in which Paul encourages Christians to continue (Rom 12:10; 1 Thess 4:9-11; cf. 1 Pet 3:8). Refusal of love to the brother or sister is a denial of one's own filial relationship to the loving Father (1 John 3, particularly vv. 10, 14–17; 4:7-12, 20-21). The New Testament epistles generally restrict the brotherhood to the circle of believers. But all human beings, made in the divine image, are called to filial communion with God and should therefore be considered by Christians as future brothers and sisters at least. This squares with Jesus' injunction to love the—temporary—enemy (Matt 5:43-48) and his vision of the neighbor to be loved as any person in need (Luke 10:25-37). It is also in harmony with Jesus' creative action in sharing table-fellowship with sinners (e.g., Luke 15).

As the body of Christ, the Church is revealed to be a liturgical community, for it is essentially a eucharistic community—one which celebrates the memory of Christ by eating and drinking the bread and wine become his body and blood, thereby becoming the very body of Christ. The celebration of the Eucharist was established for the Church as the constitutive sign of its union with the Lord who gives his life for the life of the world. In the Eucharist, Christ appears as God's supreme gift to us, God's own Son, the beloved; and, in response, the Eucharistic Prayer itself is a memorial thanksgiving for that gift of Christ *in illo tempore*. In the Communion, Christ comes to us again as God's self-gift *hic et nunc* and we are enabled in response to offer ourselves to God. In the light of God's self-gift in Christ we are able to see all the other benefactions of God towards us: all is gift. From the side of humankind, Christ's total surrender of himself in love towards God and towards friend, neighbor, and enemy ("Father, forgive them") defines a moment into which we must enter if we are to fulfill the human vocation to communion/friendship with God and among ourselves.

The eucharistic community sees and joys in God's self-giving love and incarnate saving will in Jesus Christ. The Holy Spirit of that love which is the life of the eucharistic community enables that community to share its joyful vision of God's love with outsiders: "By this all persons will know that you are my disciples, if you have love for one another" (John 13:35). The mutual love/friendship of the eucharistic community is the sacrament of God's beauty, revealing the splendor and communicating the joy of God's love to the world. Such love enables the world to know that Christ has loved his disciples, because it is the expression of his imperative/call to love, "even as I have loved you" (John 13:34). Their loving communion is the gift of God: "The glory which you have given me I have given to them, that they may be one even as we are one" (John 17:22). They now radiate the "glory" or beauty of God's love and joy.

## Scripture and Liturgy

The purpose of the Bible for the Christian community is the communion of the community with God who gives Godself to us in Christ and the Holy Spirit. Through the prayerful contemplation of its Scriptures, the Church hears God's voice and message, and from its own side, the Church responds to God in prayer. The holiness of the Scriptures derives from both their source and their function. They mediate the word of God, their author, who assists our understanding and application of them. They come to us from the past as witnessing the definitive revelation of God; it is by their means that the definitive revelation is able to qualify our present.

The Old Testament liturgy brought into focus the continuing benefits of an earlier and foundational act of salvation: it allowed people to thank God for the original act and for the blessings which by God's doing continued to flow from it. In the case of the harvest festival, for example, the first fruits are representative of the whole crop. It allowed people to commit themselves afresh to this God and to a way of life which conformed to God's spirit and will (e.g., Deut 26:10-19; Josh 24:14-28). It was the function of narrative recital, and later of the Scriptures into which it became incorporated, to recall the inaugural saving event. The matter was understood in terms of the continuing identity of God and the people. The same God who once brought the people into the Promised Land then continued to give its blessings to successive generations. If they were to retain their identity as the favored people, the succeeding generations had for their part to renew the commitment their ancestors made to the God of their salvation. The liturgy was, and *mutatis mutandis* remains for us, the locus in which the story of the constitutive events is retold in order to elicit an appropriate response in worship and ethics to the God who remains faithful to the purposes which God's earlier acts declared. As the book in which the original stories have been deposited, developed, and classically defined, the Scriptures subserve that continuing function of the liturgy.

The liturgical element in the New Testament appears in the adaptations and applications of earlier traditions made necessary by differences in cultural circumstances. The Gospels proclaim the Christian message in terms appropriate to particular situations. Mark's Gospel is "rewritten" by Luke because the delay in the expected parousia obliges him to place the Christian community in "salvation history," and by Matthew in order to reach the special problems of his Jewish-Christian context. The process of preaching the Christian message in terms appropriate to particular situations had already begun before any of our New Testament documents were written. Many of the gospel pericopes had been used in the earliest preaching of the Church, evidencing the broadly "liturgical" character of the New Testament material. Confessions of faith in Jesus Christ as Lord or Son of God also reflect liturgical usage. Whether in acclamatory or in creedal form, these confessions of faith are made not only to God but also to the world; for Christ's domain is not only the Church but the world. The Church discloses to the world the truth about itself.

The hymn is another liturgical form of the New Testament. New Testament writers employed the known hymns of the Christian community to establish points of doctrine (e.g., Col 1:15-20). Prayers are another form of liturgical material to be found in the New Testament. The Lord's Prayer is a paradigm for Christian worship. Other liturgical material is provided by the norms given for various liturgical occasions. New Testament writers draw upon the recognized liturgical practice of the community when they are establishing points of doctrine or give ethical teaching (e.g., Rom 6; 1 Cor 1:13; Gal 3:26-29).

The liturgy contributed decisively to the structuring of whole books or series of books in the Bible. The liturgy contributed to the content, composition, establishment, delimitation, and doctrinal use of the Church's Scriptures. The liturgy is the primary context for the Church's understanding and use of Scriptures.

The constant reading of the Scriptures in the liturgy evidences that Christianity considers itself a historical religion based upon the revelation of God in Jesus Christ and his community of faith. From the start, Christians interpreted Jesus as the fulfillment of the promises made by God to Israel and, through Israel, to the world. Christians claimed the Jewish Scriptures as their own Scriptures. Their use in Christian worship signifies their original and continuing function of providing an interpretative framework for the history of Jesus. The earliest Christian understandings of Jesus, in the context of Israel and Graeco-Roman culture, became deposited in the writings which eventually attained the status of New Testament Scripture. By the time of the late second century, the chief formal criterion of a writing's acceptability for reading in church was its apostolic origin. The Church of the first centuries looked to the apostles for the authorized account and interpretation of the story of Jesus, his person, his teaching, and the events surrounding him. This has been the continuing justification for the reading of the New Testament in Christian worship.

The liturgical reading of Scripture bears witness to the Church's traditional concern for its historical foundation in Jesus. Two themes mark the Church's concern: the concern for who Jesus was, what he said, did and suffered, and the concern for the apostolic witness to him. The two are inseparably linked, for the second is a means of access to the first.

The story of Jesus had been told, interpreted, and applied in rapidly changing circumstances before it was deposited in the New Testament writings. Historically, the New Testament Scriptures supply our closest witness in time to Jesus and to the impact he had. It is part of the ministry of teaching in the Church to help

Christian worshipers know their Lord through the liturgical use of its Scriptures. The Church's use of Scriptures in the context of worship both expresses and confirms our trust that God has provided for us an adequate foundational record—however *chiaroscuro* in mode—of God's self-revelation in Christ.

The normative/canonical function of the Scriptures throughout the history of the Church safeguards the substance of Christianity. The liturgy provides a continuing context for the positive interpretation of Scripture. This is important for the organic development of doctrine. The New Testament is also canonical with respect to the method for communicating its substance. The New Testament writings exemplify the way the gospel is always to be preached into particular circumstances, where it will meet with a particular response. The Church's liturgy provides a focal context for that particular preaching and that appropriate response.

The liturgy indulges in considerable "cross-referencing" among the various New Testament writings. It does so at the readings by allowing the Epistle and the Gospel to comment on each other. Later Christian hymns draw on various New Testament texts. Creeds and classical prayers blend the principal themes and images of the New Testament into a total pattern. All this constitutes a liturgical basis for the traditional principle of exegesis and interpretation according to which the passages of Scripture should be allowed to illuminate one another. What all New Testament writings have in common is devotion to the person of Jesus Christ as Messiah and Lord; consequently, the variety of New Testament writings is without contradictoriness. The Christian community's worship of its Lord is the unifying/integrating principle for its use of Scriptures.

The liturgy serves as a hermeneutical continuum for the Church's Scriptures. It has contributed to the preservation and transmission of the biblical text. Before the invention of printing, it was largely to meet liturgical needs that manuscripts were copied. Liturgical use sets the proper atmosphere for the exegete and interpreter. The basic motivation of Christian exegesis and hermeneutics should be doxological. The liturgy supplies thematic guidelines for the exegete and interpreter. It composes the multiple motifs of the Scriptures into a coherent vision.

The liturgy is the preeminent place in which the Church ponders and applies the Scriptures. It thus contributes creatively to the development of doctrine. The liturgy contributes to surmounting the historical and cultural gulf between the ancient writings and the present community. The liturgical or devotional use of the Bible accentuates its relevance to new situations in which the grace and call of God challenge the Christian community to decision and action.

The same divine guidance that inspired the composition and choice of the Church's Scriptures is also required in the case of the Church's preaching, as it seeks to interpret and apply the message of the New Testament. With regard to both Scriptures and sermon, at their proper levels, it has been traditional to speak of "divine inspiration." This inspiration has been ascribed to the Holy Spirit. The presence of the Holy Spirit implies that of God who was revealed in Jesus Christ and that of the Lord Jesus himself (e.g., John 14:8-11, 15-23). Without the divine assistance, the preacher's message will not "come alive" in the particular circumstances.

In its liturgy the Christian community has experienced the divine presence both in the reading of the Scriptures and the preaching. It believes that God is present in both God's word and in God's sacrament of the altar. In its Constitution on the Sacred Liturgy, the Second Vatican Council affirms the multiple modes of Christ's presence in the continuing work of salvation:

> To accomplish so great a work, Christ is always present in his Church, especially in its liturgical actions. He is present in the person of his minister, "the same now offering, through the ministry of priests, who formerly offered himself on the cross," but especially under the eucharistic species. By his power he is present in the sacraments, so that when a man baptizes it is really Christ himself who baptizes. He is present in his word, since it is he himself who speaks when the holy scriptures are read in church. He is present, lastly, when the Church prays and sings, for he promised: "Where two or three are gathered together in my name, there am I in the midst of them." Christ indeed always associates the Church with himself in this great work wherein God is perfectly glorified and men are sanctified.

The Christian community enjoys the beauty of its self-giving God in both God's word and sacrament of the altar. In the liturgy the Holy Spirit enables us to see and joy in the beauty of God's love. The desire and work of the Spirit in the heart of the Church and its liturgy is that we may live from the life of the risen and glorified Christ. Communion with the Holy Trinity, Beauty/Happiness Itself, and fraternal communion are inseparable in the fruit of the Spirit in the liturgy.

*   *   *

The New Testament writers attempt to capture the mysterious beauty which irradiates from the loving Son of God. The New Testament writers witness to what they have seen with the eye of faith: the Word became flesh and dwelt among us and we saw his glory (John 1:14). Jesus is the glory/beauty that he communicates. His glory/beauty is seen only by those whose eyes have been illuminated by the light which radiates from him, who are drawn into the reality of his supreme goodness. The church, living out its life in worship and practice, mediates what it sees/contemplates of God's glory/beauty in Jesus Christ. The Church's Scriptures are an account of the new existence into which those who see the glory/beauty are transported.

# 13

# Radiant Spirit

The Holy Spirit communicates the beauty of God's goodness at the creation of the world and in the new creation that is Jesus Christ and his community of faith. The Spirit brings the existing world out of the primordial void, creating cosmos out of chaos (Gen 1:2). God promises to bring the people up out of their graves, to recreate Israel: "And I will put my spirit in you, and you shall live" (Ezek 37:1-14). The conception, birth, and life of Jesus bear witness to the promised new creation. Jesus is "full of the Holy Spirit" (Luke 4:1). He possesses the power of the Holy Spirit and acts in that power (Luke 4:14). He is not the mere object of the Spirit's activity. Jesus sends his Spirit (Luke 24:49; Acts 2:33); therefore, he is not subordinated to it. Jesus' sending of his Spirit to the disciples at Pentecost constitutes the birth of the Church, when the Spirit becomes the ever-present reality within the Church (Acts 2:1). The Church lives under the rule of Jesus Christ the Lord, who governs the hearts and minds of its members through his Holy Spirit. The activities of the Holy Spirit of love and truth are especially outgoing, both in impelling evangelism (Acts 8:29; 16:6) and in equipping the evangelist (Acts 4:8; 6:5; 13:9). The beauty of the risen Christ's love and truth inspire the joyful communication of the Good News. Evangelism is the Spirit of that love, truth, joy, and beauty in action, transforming human minds and hearts, inspiring decision and action, transfiguring the world.

Through the gift of the Spirit, we are enabled to see and relish the beauty of God in Jesus Christ. The Holy Spirit endows us with the love that is "the eye" of faith and "the look" of Christian contemplation, enabling our joyful experience of communion, community, and communication with Beauty Itself (God) in the body of Christ and in the temple of his Spirit. God reveals God's very beauty through and in the Spirit of God's love. Without the Spirit it is impossible to see and joy in the beauty of God.

The New England theologian Jonathan Edwards affirmed that God's beauty is preeminent among God's attributes: God is beauty itself, the source and foundation of all beauty in the world.[1] He states that the Father created the world with the Son, and that the Holy Spirit, being the harmony, excellence, and beauty of the deity, has the particular function of communicating beauty and harmony in the world.[2] This function follows from the Spirit's role within the Trinity, where the Father and the Son delight in each other, and breathe forth the Holy Spirit in love and joy. Hence, the Holy Spirit, being the love and joy of God, is God's beauty and happiness, and it is in our partaking of the same Holy Spirit that our communion with God consists.[3] Edwards is here taking the Augustinian view of the Holy Spirit as proceeding from the Father and the Son, and as the harmony or bond of love between them. God's beauty, for Edwards, is the beauty of this love, of the Spirit of the Father and Son.

The Holy Spirit has three functions, for Edwards, with regard to creatures: to enliven and beautify all things; to sanctify intelligent beings by communicating God's love (which the Spirit is) to them; and as the Comforter to comfort and delight the hearts of God's people.[4] He interprets the first function in the light of

---

[1] Jonathan Edwards, *A Treatise Concerning Religious Affections,* ed. John E. Smith (New Haven, 1959) 265, 298. Roland Delattre's *Beauty and Sensibility in the Thought of Jonathan Edwards* (New Haven, Conn., 1968) is a very comprehensive and helpful treatment of Edwards' thought here.

[2] Jonathan Edwards, *Miscellaneous Observations on Important Theological Subjects,* ed. John Erskine (Edinburgh, 1793) 434. J. Edwards, *Miscellanies,* 293. *The Philosophy of Jonathan Edwards, from his Private Notebooks,* ed. Harvey G. Townsend (Westport, Conn., 1972) 260.

[3] J. Edwards, *Essay on the Trinity,* ed. George P. Fisher (New York, 1903) 108.

[4] Ibid., 97–102.

Genesis 1:2, which he glosses to read "the Spirit of God moved
upon the face of the waters or of the Chaos to bring it out of its
Confusion into harmony and beauty," and by quoting Job 26:13,
which he translates as "God by his Spirit garnished the heavens";
and he concludes, "whose office can it be so Properly to give all
things their sweetness and beauty as he who is himself beauty and
Joy of the Creator."[5] Thus the Holy Spirit communicates God's
love and beauty to the world, transfiguring it with the joy of the
Creator.

The Holy Spirit's two functions of beautifying and sanctifying
are identical for Edwards; for God's beauty is God's holiness, and
our sanctification is the most significant manifestation of our participation in God's beauty.[6]

Edwards does not associate the divine beauty with the Holy
Spirit alone, for he recognizes the Son, too, as the image of God's
glory, and therefore as manifesting God's beauty. Filled with the
beauty of the Holy Spirit, Jesus attracts people. Edwards states in
one of his sermons that "it is this sight of the divine beauty in
Christ, that bows the wills, and draws the hearts of men."[7] In the
same sermon he says that it is the saving grace of God's Spirit that
enables us to apprehend the divine beauty.[8] In another sermon he
says that the light of the Holy Spirit, which is "a kind of emana-
tion of God's beauty," gives a "sense of the heart" whereby the
saints discover "the divine superlative glory and excellency of
God and Christ."[9] The divine beauty that is the Holy Spirit appears in the Son.[10]

Edwards explains that God is glorified within Godself in two
ways, by being manifested in God's own perfect idea, the Son,
and by delighting in Godself by flowing forth in the Holy Spirit

[5] Ibid., 98.
[6] Ibid., 97.
[7] J. Edwards, "True Grace Distinguished from the Experience of Devils,"
in *Works,* Bohn edn., ii (London, 1865) 49.
[8] Ibid., 48.
[9] J. Edwards, "A Divine and Supernatural Light, Immediately imparted to
the Soul by the Spirit of God, shown to be both a Scriptural and Rational
Doctrine." Ibid., 15–16.
[10] Roland Delattre, *Beauty and Sensibility,* 156.

in infinite love and delight towards Godself. Likewise, God glorifies Godself towards creatures in two ways, by being manifested in their understanding, and by communicating God's very self to their hearts and wills. Thus, he says, "God is glorified not only by his glory's being seen, but by its being rejoiced in."[11] God communicates God's very self through the gift of the Holy Spirit to beautify creation and to transform human minds and hearts. Through the gift of the Holy Spirit we participate in the delight, love, and joy of the Father and Son. The Holy Spirit gives all things their sweetness and beauty which comes from its being the beauty of the Creator's joy.[12] We participate in the beauty and joy of God to the extent that we welcome God's Holy Spirit into our lives.

If the world's beauty and harmony is both the gift and a participation in the divine beauty and harmony, then its beauty and harmony depend on the presence and activity of the Holy Spirit. The love and peace and harmony of the disciples offer incontestable evidence of Christ and his Holy Spirit: "By this all men will know that you are my disciples, if you have love for one another" (John 13:35).

Edwards' theology of the Holy Spirit and beauty is in the tradition of Augustine, Aquinas, and Bonaventure. Aquinas, for example, also finds harmony and joy appropriate to the Holy Spirit because the Spirit proceeds from the other two Persons and is the bond between them, and because they joyfully rest in each other (*ST* Ia, q. 39, a. 8).

Theologizing in the same tradition, Frederick Crowe affirms that the Spirit is Love and love is first of all a peace and harmony and rest in the enjoyment of what is, and then it is an unrest and a desire and striving for what can and should be.[13] All this, the Spirit is in God. It is God's eternal personal "character." This, therefore, is what the Spirit will be in the world, that is to say, the Spirit will represent acceptance of what is and harmony with the

---

[11] J. Edwards, *Miscellanies,* 448.

[12] J. Edwards, *Essay on the Trinity,* 93–4, 98.

[13] Frederick Crowe, "The Doctrine of the Most Holy Trinity," informally published class notes (Willowdale, Ont., 1965–1966) 192.

universe of being. The Spirit will find this role in relation to that of the Son, bringing us to the truth, not as the revealer of new truth but as hearing and welcoming the Son with love. Furthermore, as representing the divine unrest, the Spirit will be the principle of development, keeping the freshness of youth in the Church and society and continuously renewing them (Vatican II, *De Ecclesia,* c. 1). So whatever pertains to these aspects will be part of the theology of the Spirit in the world and the "logical" extension of the treatise on grace and charity: affectivity, peace, unity, communion, community, communications, interpersonal and social life, prayer life, and the like.[14]

The Holy Spirit is the principle of perpetual rejuvenation in the divinization of the world. Crowe stresses the fact that the only God there is, is the triune God, who communicates this life to us as triune, and therefore the divinization of the human world is really its "trinification."[15] The Trinity in the world gives, therefore, something like a permanent structure to its new creation. Christian life will be a pilgrimage to the Father, with the truth of the Son to give us security, and the love of the Spirit to motivate us. But within these structural lines there will always be change, development, and the emergence of new forms. Although such change is to be expected in the life and institutions of the historical beings that we are, we have to relate it to the permanency of the triune God's self-giving structure.[16] If to be made in the image and likeness of God implies that human activity works in the likeness of the divine, then we have in the triune God the motive and pattern for balancing our concerns and striving with a basic peace and contentment.

If God is love, then the primary referent for the meaning of love is God's very self and the way in which the Church both knows and experiences God as love is in the reality of the Trinity. Love which constitutes the essence of the divine self-communication

---

[14] Ibid., 193.

[15] Ibid., 178.

[16] Ibid. 193. Crowe affirms that the Holy Spirit stands for our acceptance of the word of God and for harmony with all that it is, but what we are is largely potential, so the Holy Spirit stands also for the emergence of new understanding and new forms in the Church (194).

upon which the Church is based has a trinitarian structure: a dynamic, eternally creative, relational ontology constitutive of divine being.[17] As Trinity, God is *Amor Amans,* or the life which takes place in the internal self-communication (the dynamic loving or *perichoresis*) between the Father, the Son, and the Holy Spirit. It is this love and life which God makes available to us as healing and redemption in Jesus and in the sending of the Holy Spirit of love. The heavenly Father reaches out to humankind through the body of the Son and the temple of the Spirit to take it into the eternal life, love, joy, and beauty of the divine triune communion (Trinity).

If the Father is the beginning and the Son is the culmination of salvation history, then the Holy Spirit of their love is its universalization.[18] Jesus himself described the Holy Spirit, whom he was to mission and who would thus be his (Christ's) mission, as "another Paraclete" (John 14:16). The history of the world after Pentecost is truly the history of the Holy Spirit, in whose powerful communion we come to appreciate and understand better the triune God, who is with us always to the end of time (Matt 28:20). The Spirit of the triune God's love is without limits; it is the Spirit "who blows wherever it pleases. . . . You cannot tell where it comes from or where it is going" (John 3:8). The Holy Spirit radiates the beauty of the triune God's universal love that transfigures the world. It brings the joy and splendor of God's self-giving love into the very heart of the world and to its very ends (Rom 5:5 with Acts 1:8). The joy and beauty of the divine triune communion/ love renews the face of the earth (Ps 104:30) in the outpouring of the Holy Spirit.

Peace expresses one aspect of how the Holy Spirit beautifies the world. In the ancient Church, a synonym for communion was peace.[19] In fact, they often appeared together as a doublet. "Peace" alone often indicated the community, the communion of the saints, the Church, united by the Holy Spirit of love. According to

---

[17] James Hanvey, "Believing in the Church," *The Month* (Feb. 1995) 48.

[18] Robert Kress, *The Church: Communion, Sacrament, Communication* (New York: Paulist, 1985) 33.

[19] Ibid., 36.

St. Paul, "Christ . . . is the peace between us (Jews and Gentiles), and has made the two into one and broken down the barriers which used to separate them, actually destroying in his person the hostility . . . to create one single new man in himself out of the two of them and by restoring peace . . . to unite them both in a single body and reconcile them with God. In his own person . . . he came to bring the good news of peace, peace to you who were far away and peace to those who were near at hand. Through him, both of us have in the one Spirit our way to come to the Father" (Eph 2:13-18). This peace, which happens in Jesus, is communion —of God with humankind and of humans among themselves. This peace does not cease with the earthly ministry of Jesus. Rather, in the Holy Spirit he has given us a lasting *way* to the Father. Not only is Jesus "the Way, the Truth, and the Life" (John 14:6); so is the Church, according to Paul: "It is according to the way which they describe as a sect that I worship the God of my ancestors . . ." (Acts 24:14; also 9:2; 16:17; 18:25-26; 19:9, 23; 22:4; 24:22). This passage from Ephesians locates ecclesial communion precisely in the triune communion. The love which is the eye of Christian faith and the look/vision of Christian contemplation evidences our life in the Holy Spirit of both the ecclesial and triune communion. Both Christian faith and contemplation manifest the way the peace of the Holy Spirit transfigures humankind through the gift of God's love. The "Alternative Opening Prayer" for the feast of All Saints synthesizes key aspects of the Triune God, Beauty Itself, at work in beautifying creation:

> God our Father,
> source of all holiness,
> the work of your hands is manifest in your saints,
> the beauty of your truth is reflected in their faith.
> May we who aspire to have part in their joy
> be filled with the Spirit that blessed their lives,
> so that having shared their faith on earth
> we may also know their peace in your kingdom.[20]

[20] *The Weekday Missal, A New Edition* (London: Collins Liturgical Publications, 1987) 1761.

The eschatological role of the Holy Spirit's beautifying the world is affirmed by Leonid Ouspensky: "True beauty is the radiance of the Holy Spirit, the holiness of and the participation in the life of the world to come."[21] He goes on to say that icons of the saints remind us of their holiness and so serve as "a revelation of the holiness of the world to come, a plan and a project of the cosmic transfiguration."[22] The Russian Orthodox theologian Sergius Bulgakov reaffirms the eschatological role of the Holy Spirit, found in some of the early Fathers of the Church, as the Perfecter: "God is glorious, and His Glory is Beauty itself." He then says that the Father gave existence to the world through the Son, and completes it through the Holy Spirit; and that at the end of time the heavenly Jerusalem will come, and "the whole world, too, the waters and the land, will be transfigured by the Holy Ghost, and will appear in their beauty."[23] Wolterstorff argues that "aesthetic delight is a component within and a species of that joy which belongs to the shalom God has ordained as the goal of human existence."[24] The joy that radiates from God's beauty/love is even now a proleptic experience of the eternal happiness that God has predestined for all who love God. It is always the gift/fruit of the Holy Spirit of God's love (Gal 5:22; Rom 14:17; 1 Thess 1:6).

John F. Haught interprets our experience of the eschatological tension that is human longing and restlessness in terms of beauty: "that ultimately satisfying beauty for which we long but which continues to elude us is what the word 'God' means," and suggests that God may be thought of as the horizon of ultimate beauty towards which we are irresistibly drawn.[25] Bonaventure held that since God alone is goodness and beauty itself, only in

[21] Leonid Ouspensky, *Theology of the Icon* (Crestwood, N.Y., 1978) 190.

[22] Ibid., 228.

[23] Sergius Bulgakov, "Religion and Art," *The Church of God: An Anglo-Russian Symposium,* ed. E. L. Mascall (London, 1934) 175–6. See also his *Le Paraclet* (Paris, 1946), especially ch. 4, where he describes the beauty of the world as the created effect of the Holy Spirit; and Charles Lee Graves, *The Holy Spirit in the Theology of Sergius Bulgakov* (Geneva, 1972) ch. 2.

[24] Nicholas Wolterstorff, *Art in Action: Toward a Christian Aesthetic* (Grand Rapids, 1980) 169.

[25] John Haught, *What is God?* (New York: Paulist Press, 1986) 70.

God is there perfect delight.[26] All created beauty expresses the gift and call of its Creator to the perfect delight that is Happiness Itself/Beauty Itself/ Love Itself.

The transfiguration of Christ discloses the power and mission of the Transfigured for the transfiguration of all humankind. The glory of the risen Christ anticipates the glory of all who share his invincible Holy Spirit of love which has conquered death itself. Paul describes the risen Christ as the first-born among many brethren (Rom 8:29). The brethren share his life, the Spirit of love, which neither sin nor death itself can quench. The joy of the brethren, even now, radiates the beauty of the Spirit of the Father's love that raised Jesus from the dead: "If the Spirit of him who raised Jesus from the dead is living in you, then he who raised Jesus from the dead will give life to your own mortal bodies through his Spirit living in you" (Rom 8:11).

In Christ's resurrection the three divine Persons act together as one, and manifest their own proper characteristics.[27] The Father's power "raised up" Christ the Son and by doing so perfectly introduced the Son's humanity, including his body, into the splendor of the Trinity. Jesus is conclusively revealed as "Son of God in power according to the Spirit of holiness by his resurrection from the dead" (Rom 1:3-4; Acts 2:24). Paul insists on the manifestation of God's power (Rom 6:4; 2 Cor 13:4) through the working of the Spirit who gave life to Jesus' dead humanity and called it to the glorious state of Lordship. At Jesus' resurrection his body is filled with the power of the Holy Spirit: he shares the divine life in his glorious state, so that Paul can say that Christ is "the man of heaven" (1 Cor 15:35-50).

The Church is constituted in the life of the Trinity and, moreover, by her very existence bears witness to the triune reality of love. The trinitarian essence of the Church which makes faith in God inseparable from God's work of establishing and sustaining God's community, also locates the Church in humankind and its openness to God's transfiguring presence in history. All human-

---

[26] Bonaventure (i *Sent.* i. 3.2; Quaracchi edn., i, 41).

[27] *Catechism of the Catholic Church,* Pocket Edition (London: Geoffrey Chapman, 1995) 648.

kind is orientated and in search of the eschatological goal of history itself, the divine glory or beauty, which we even now know through grace to be the triune communion, community, and communications of love. The Church is not just life *from* God but life *with* God and as such the community for all humankind. It is the temple of the Holy Spirit for beautifying humankind in the glory of God's love.

The Spirit of God's love that beautifies humankind is always the Spirit of God's joy. Jesus, at his departure, sends his disciples back in joy (Luke 24:52-53); they are to bear his joy to the world. The words of the gospel (Acts 8:8; 13:48), like baptism (Acts 8:39; 13:52) and faith itself (Acts 16:34), fill the Church with joy. In joy and purity of heart the community of Christian faith celebrates the eucharistic banquet (Acts 2:46). Joy marks the presence of the Lord experienced at the banquet, through which presence their ultimate communion with God is anticipated. In joy the missionaries render service (Acts 8:39; 11:23). The apostle serves the joy of the Church (2 Cor 1:24), and at the same time he shares in her joy (Rom 16:19; Phil 2:17-18).

The foundation for joy is the love of the Father, who has established the Church in the kingdom of the beloved Son (Col 1:12-13). The Christian community radiates "joy in the Lord" (Phil 3:1; 4:4) and "joy in the Holy Spirit" (Luke 10:21; Acts 13:52; Rom 14:17; 1 Thess 1:6). As the presence of God, the Holy Spirit is the basic cause of joy (Gal 5:22). Christ, anointed with the oil of joy on account of his righteousness, is the foundation of the joy among his disciples (Heb 1:9).[28]

The joy of the Church is experienced in its faith (Phil 1:25), hope (Rom 12:12; 15:13), love (1 Cor 13:6; Gal 5:22), consolation (Acts 15:31), peace (Rom 14:17; 15:13; Gal 5:22), truth (1 Cor

---

[28] We read in the Old Testament that God delights in Israel (Isa 62:5); God rejoices in God's works (Ps 104:32). The activity of God in history is cause for joy (Ps 98:4). Peace and joy go together (Rom 14:17; 15:33; 16:20; Gal 5:22). *Shalom* (peace) combines the notion of well-being and contentment with joy (e.g., Lev 26:6; Ps 85:9-14). Peace and joy are messianic-eschatological concepts. The Messiah is the "Prince of Peace" (Isa 9:6) who brings the joy, kindness, and glory/beauty of God (Isa 45:8, 17, 24–25).

13:6), prayer (1 Thess 5:16; Phil 1:4), thanksgiving (Col 1:11), service of love (2 Cor 8:2; 9:7).

Joy, like the Holy Spirit of joy, is indestructible. The joy of the disciples remains in spite of affliction (John 16:20). Paul experiences "abundant joy in the midst of affliction" (2 Cor 7:4). The Christians in Thessalonica accepted the word with the joy of the Holy Spirit, despite their afflictions (1 Thess 1:6). The invincible joy of Christians is the promise of eschatological joy: "Rejoice and be glad, for your reward is great in heaven" (Matt 5:12). The Lord is even now calling God's faithful servants into God's joy (Matt 25:21-23). The present joy of the Church is the promise and assurance of future glory (John 16:20, 22). It is evidence that the Church experiences the radiant beauty of the Holy Spirit's transfiguring love; for the reality of love, truth, goodness felt is beauty.[29]

The prayer of the Church affirms that God is working out our eternal happiness, even now, through the beauty of human life and creation:

> God our Father,
> open our eyes to see your hand at work
> in the splendor of creation,
> in the beauty of human life.
> Touched by your hand our world is holy.
> Help us to cherish the gifts that surround
> us, to share your blessings with our
> brothers and sisters, and to experience
> the joy of life in your presence.
> We ask this through Christ our Lord. Amen.[30]

Jesus' giving sight to the blind is a metaphor for his giving us the Holy Spirit of his love which enables our enjoyment of God's beauty in Christian faith (the eye of love) and contemplation (the look of love).[31] He gives us the Holy Spirit of life, love, joy, truth,

---

[29] Sergius Bulgakov, *Le Paraclet,* 176. What Bulgakov says beauty does for truth also holds for love and goodness.

[30] The "Alternative Opening Prayer" for Sunday, 30 July 1995 (Sunday in Ordinary Time).

[31] For Aquinas, in the present life the utmost happiness takes the form of contemplation (*Summa contra Gentes* 3.37). It is a loving awareness of the

and peace in the triune communion-community-communications that beautifies all creation as the origin-ground-perfection of its beauty. Through the gift of the Holy Spirit's new creation, we enjoy the beauty of God in all creation.[32]

## Four Ways the Holy Spirit Beautifies Humankind

The Holy Spirit creates a beauty in humankind that we could not enjoy without it. The Holy Spirit of love beautifies humankind in ways that transcend our human limitations. The Spirit manifests this beauty in our forgiving the humanly unforgivable; in our hoping in apparent hopelessness; in our joy in the apparent absence of the enjoyable; in our loving in the apparent absence of the lovable.

Just as our prayer bespeaks the Spirit's praying within us, our forgiving the unforgivable bespeaks the Spirit's forgiving within us. Similarly, our hoping in apparent hopelessness bespeaks the Spirit's hoping within us. Our joy in the apparent absence of the enjoyable bespeaks the Spirit's joy within us. Our loving in the apparent absence of the humanly lovable bespeaks the Spirit's loving within us. Our forgiving, hoping, joy, and love in these circumstances manifest the transcendent and invincible love that is the Holy Spirit of the Father and Son. Jesus' Way of the Cross in confronting evil is the way of God's invincible love culminating in the resurrection. The compelling beauty of that Love saves the world.

---

divine ground of the universe, the basis for festivity or having "a good time," according to Josef Pieper in his theory of festivity: *In Tune with the World*, trans. R. and C. Winston (New York: Harcourt, Brace & World, Inc., 1965) 13. Our happiness is only as great as our capacity for contemplation, our loving gaze on the beloved, according to Pieper in *Josef Pieper: An Anthology* (San Francisco: Ignatius Press, 1989) 143. See also J. Pieper, *Happiness and Contemplation* (New York, 1958).

[32] The reason for joy, although it may be encountered in a myriad of concrete forms, is always the same: possessing or receiving what one loves, whether actually in the present, hoped for in the future, or remembered in the past (Aquinas, *ST* I–II, q. 2, a. 6). Joy is an expression of love. One who loves nobody and nothing cannot possibly rejoice, no matter how much one craves joy. Joy is always the response of a lover welcoming what he or she loves. See J. Pieper, *In Tune With the World*, 17–8.

Printed in the United States
213337BV00001B/4/A